ΣΟΦΟΚΛΕΟΥΣ Οιδίπους ἐπὶ Κολωνῷ

SOPHOCLES' *Oedipus at Colonus*

A Dual Language Edition

Greek Text Edited by
Sir Richard Jebb

English Translation and Notes by
Ian Johnston

Edited by
Evan Hayes and Stephen Nimis

FAENUM PUBLISHING
OXFORD, OHIO

Sophocles Oedipus at Colonus*: A Dual Language Edition*
First Edition

ISBN-10: 1940997895
ISBN-13: 9781940997896

Published by Faenum Publishing, Ltd.
Cover Design: Evan Hayes

for Geoffrey (1974-1997)

οἵη περ φύλλων γενεὴ τοίη δὲ καὶ ἀνδρῶν.
φύλλα τὰ μέν τ' ἄνεμος χαμάδις χέει, ἄλλα δέ θ' ὕλη
τηλεθόωσα φύει, ἔαρος δ' ἐπιγίγνεται ὥρη:
ὣς ἀνδρῶν γενεὴ ἣ μὲν φύει ἣ δ' ἀπολήγει.

Generations of men are like the leaves.
In winter, winds blow them down to earth,
but then, when spring season comes again,
the budding wood grows more. And so with men:
one generation grows, another dies away. (*Iliad* 6)

TABLE OF CONTENTS

EDITORS' NOTE

This volume presents the Ancient Greek text of Sophocles' *Oedipus at Colonus* with a facing English translation. The Greek text is that of Richard Jebb, which is in the public domain and available as a pdf. This text has also been digitized by the Perseus Project (perseus.tufts.edu). The English translation and accompanying notes are those of Ian Johnston of Vancouver Island University, Nanaimo, BC. This translation is available freely online (records.viu.ca/~johnstoi/). We have reset both texts, making a number of very minor corrections and modifications, and placed them on opposing pages. This facing-page format will be useful to those wishing to read the English translation while looking at version of the Greek original, or vice versa.

Occasionally readings from other editions of or commentaries on Sophocles ' Greek text are used, accounting for some minor departures from Jebb. Even so, some small discrepancies exist between the Greek text and the English translation.

MYTHOLOGICAL BACKGROUND

After Oedipus, king of Thebes, overwhelmed with horror at the discovery that he had killed his father and married his mother, stabbed out his eyes, he eventually left Thebes as a blind wanderer, accompanied by his daughter Antigone (there are differing accounts of when and why he left the city). Since Oedipus' two sons, Eteocles and Polyneices, were too young to take over, Creon, the brother of Oedipus' wife and mother (Jocasta, who had committed suicide), ruled Thebes as regent. Sophocles' play opens many years later. Oedipus' wanderings have brought him and Antigone to Colonus, a short distance from Athens, where there is a grove sacred to the Furies, the goddesses of blood revenge, also known as the Kindly Ones (the Eumenides).

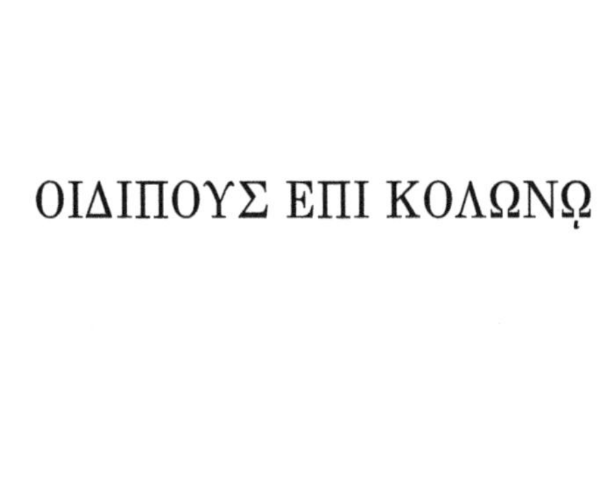

ΟΙΔΙΠΟΥΣ ΕΠΙ ΚΟΛΩΝΩ

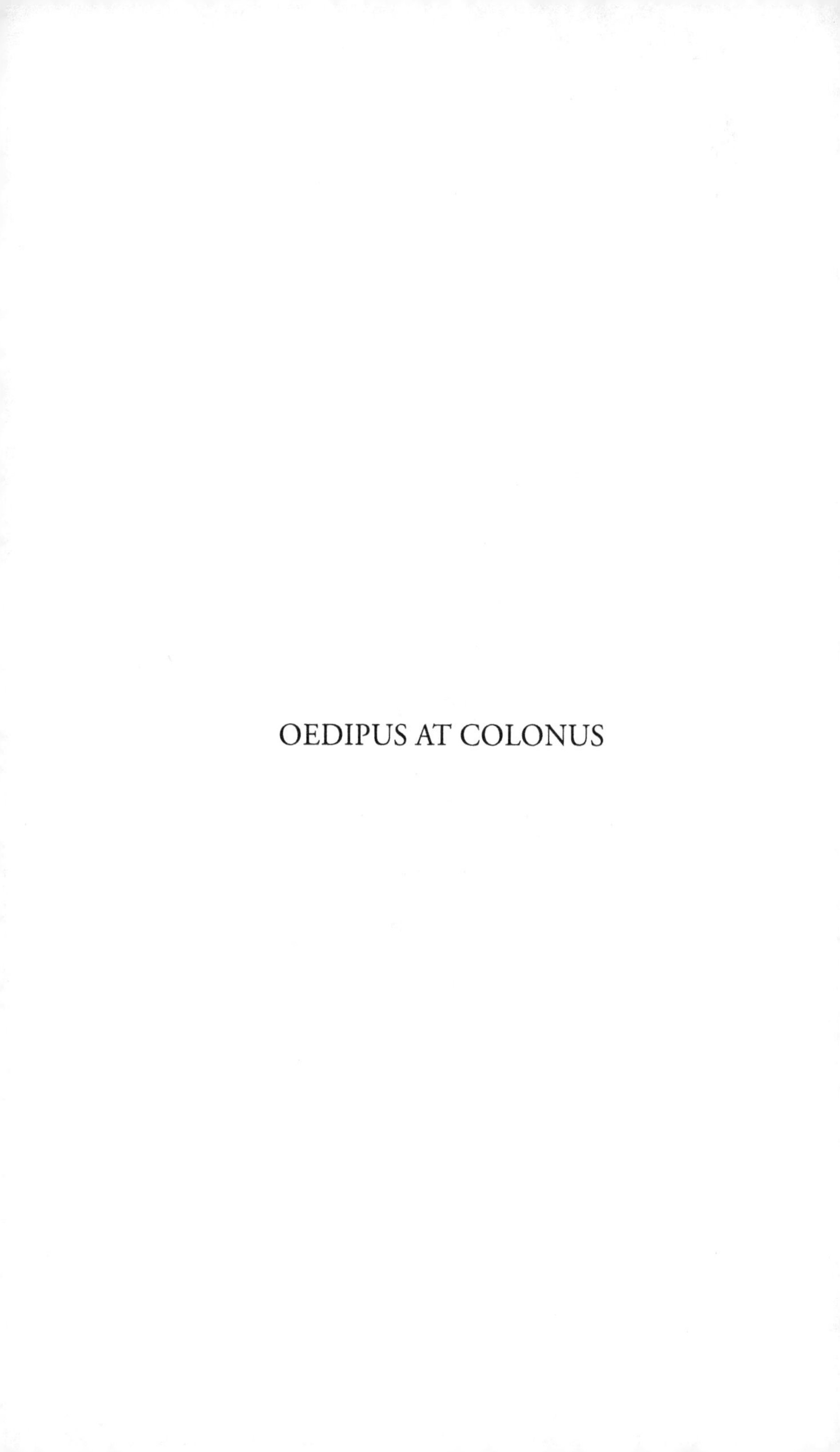

OEDIPUS AT COLONUS

ΤΑ ΤΟΥ ΔΡΑΜΑΤΟΣ ΠΡΟΣΩΠΑ

ΟΙΔΙΠΟΥΣ

ΑΝΤΙΓΟΝΕ

ΙΣΜΗΝΗ

ΘΗΣΕΥΣ

ΚΡΕΩΝ

ΠΟΛΥΝΕΙΚΗΣ

ΞΕΝΟΣ

ΑΓΓΕΛΟΣ

ΧΟΡΟΣ

DRAMATIS PERSONAE

OEDIPUS: exiled king of Thebes, an old blind wanderer

ANTIGONE: daughter of Oedipus

ISMENE: daughter of Oedipus

THESEUS: king of Athens

CREON: regent at Thebes, brother of Oedipus' dead wife, Jocasta

POLYNEICES: elder son of Oedipus

STRANGER: a citizen of Colonus

MESSENGER: a servant of Theseus

CHORUS: elderly citizens of Colonus.

Οἰδίπους ἐπὶ Κολωνῷ

Οιδιπους

τέκνον τυφλοῦ γέροντος Ἀντιγόνη, τίνας
χώρους ἀφίγμεθ' ἢ τίνων ἀνδρῶν πόλιν;
τίς τὸν πλανήτην Οἰδίπουν καθ' ἡμέραν
τὴν νῦν σπανιστοῖς δέξεται δωρήμασιν;
σμικρὸν μὲν ἐξαιτοῦντα, τοῦ σμικροῦ δ' ἔτι
μεῖον φέροντα, καὶ τόδ' ἐξαρκοῦν ἐμοί·
στέργειν γὰρ αἱ πάθαι με χὼ χρόνος ξυνὼν
μακρὸς διδάσκει καὶ τὸ γενναῖον τρίτον.
ἀλλ', ὦ τέκνον, θάκησιν εἴ τινα βλέπεις
ἢ πρὸς βεβήλοις ἢ πρὸς ἄλσεσιν θεῶν,
στῆσόν με κἀξίδρυσον, ὡς πυθώμεθα
ὅπου ποτ' ἐσμέν· μανθάνειν γὰρ ἥκομεν
ξένοι πρὸς ἀστῶν, ἃν δ' ἀκούσωμεν τελεῖν.

Αντιγονη

πάτερ ταλαίπωρ' Οἰδίπους, πύργοι μέν, οἳ
πόλιν στέγουσιν, ὡς ἀπ' ὀμμάτων, πρόσω·
χῶρος δ' ὅδ' ἱερός, ὡς ἀπεικάσαι, βρύων
δάφνης, ἐλαίας, ἀμπέλου· πυκνόπτεροι δ'
εἴσω κατ' αὐτὸν εὐστομοῦσ' ἀηδόνες·
οὗ κῶλα κάμψον τοῦδ' ἐπ' ἀξέστου πέτρου·
μακρὰν γὰρ ὡς γέροντι προὐστάλης ὁδόν.

Οιδιπους

κάθιζέ νύν με καὶ φύλασσε τὸν τυφλόν.

Αντιγονη

χρόνου μὲν οὕνεκ' οὐ μαθεῖν με δεῖ τόδε.

Oedipus at Colonus

[The action takes place in front of a grove sacred to the Furies (the Eumenides) in Colonus, a short distance from Athens. Enter OEDIPUS, led on by ANTIGONE]

OEDIPUS

Antigone, you child of an blind old man,
what country have we reached? Whose city state?
What man will welcome wandering Oedipus
with meagre gifts today? I don't need much,
and I get even less than that small pittance.
But that's sufficient for me. My suffering,
all the long years I have been living through,
and my own noble origins have taught me
to be content with that. So, my daughter,
if you can see a place to rest somewhere
on public land or by a sacred grove,
you must lead me there and let me sit,
so we can find out where we are. We've come
as foreigners to learn from people here
and carry out whatever they may say.

ANTIGONE

O father, poor tormented Oedipus,
my eyes can glimpse, off in the distance,
walls around the city. This place, it seems,
is sacred ground clustered thick with grapevines,
with laurel and olive trees. Inside the grove
many feathered nightingales are chanting
their sweet songs. Sit down and rest your limbs
on this rough stone. For a man advanced in years
you have come a long, long way.

OEDIPUS

All right, set me there,
A man who cannot see requires help.

ANTIGONE *[helping Oedipus move]*

That is a task I do not need to learn—
not after all this time.

ΟΙΔΙΠΟΥΣ

ἔχεις διδάξαι δή μ᾽ ὅποι καθέσταμεν;

ΑΝΤΙΓΟΝΗ

τὰς γοῦν Ἀθήνας οἶδα, τὸν δὲ χῶρον οὔ.

ΟΙΔΙΠΟΥΣ

πᾶς γάρ τις ηὔδα τοῦτό γ᾽ ἡμὶν ἐμπόρων.

ΑΝΤΙΓΟΝΗ

ἀλλ᾽ ὅστις ὁ τόπος ἦ μάθω μολοῦσά ποι;

ΟΙΔΙΠΟΥΣ

ναί, τέκνον, εἴπερ ἐστί γ᾽ ἐξοικήσιμος.

ΑΝΤΙΓΟΝΗ

ἀλλ᾽ ἐστὶ μὴν οἰκητός· οἴομαι δὲ δεῖν
οὐδέν· πέλας γὰρ ἄνδρα τόνδε νῷν ὁρῶ.

ΟΙΔΙΠΟΥΣ

ἦ δεῦρο προσστείχοντα κἀξορμώμενον;

ΑΝΤΙΓΟΝΗ

καὶ δὴ μὲν οὖν παρόντα· χὤ τί σοι λέγειν
εὔκαιρόν ἐστιν, ἔννεφ᾽, ὡς ἀνὴρ ὅδε.

ΟΙΔΙΠΟΥΣ

ὦ ξεῖν᾽, ἀκούων τῆσδε τῆς ὑπέρ τ᾽ ἐμοῦ
αὑτῆς θ᾽ ὁρώσης, οὕνεχ᾽ ἡμὶν αἴσιος
σκοπὸς προσήκεις ὧν ἀδηλοῦμεν φράσαι—

ΞΕΝΟΣ

πρὶν νῦν τὰ πλείον᾽ ἱστορεῖν, ἐκ τῆσδ᾽ ἕδρας
ἔξελθ᾽· ἔχεις γὰρ χῶρον οὐχ ἁγνὸν πατεῖν.

ΟΙΔΙΠΟΥΣ

τίς δ᾽ ἔσθ᾽ ὁ χῶρος; τοῦ θεῶν νομίζεται;

Oedipus *[sitting down]*
Where are we?
Can you tell me that?

Antigone
I recognize Athens,
but not this place.

Oedipus
Well, every traveller
we met with on the road has told us that.

Antigone
Shall I go and find out what this place is called?

Oedipus
Yes, my child—if there is anyone here.

Antigone
Well, there are houses. But I don't need to leave.
I see someone nearby.

Oedipus
Is he coming here?
Approaching us?

Antigone
He's already come. Ask him
whatever seems appropriate. He's here.

[Enter the STRANGER, a citizen of Colonus]

Oedipus
O stranger, from this girl whose eyes must serve
herself and me I learn that you have come
as an auspicious messenger to us
to tell us what we do not understand.

Stranger
Before you question me at any length,
move from where you sit—it's a sacrilege
to walk upon that ground.

Oedipus
What is this place?
To which of the gods is it held sacred?

ΞΕΝΟΣ

ἄθικτος οὐδ᾽ οἰκητός· αἱ γὰρ ἔμφοβοι
θεαί σφ᾽ ἔχουσι, Γῆς τε καὶ Σκότου κόραι.

ΟΙΔΙΠΟΥΣ

τίνων τὸ σεμνὸν ὄνομ᾽ ἂν εὐξαίμην κλύων;

ΞΕΝΟΣ

τὰς πάνθ᾽ ὁρώσας Εὐμενίδας ὅ γ᾽ ἐνθάδ᾽ ἂν
εἴποι λεώς νιν· ἄλλα δ᾽ ἀλλαχοῦ καλά.

ΟΙΔΙΠΟΥΣ

ἀλλ᾽ ἵλεῳ μὲν τὸν ἱκέτην δεξαίατο·
ὡς οὐχ ἕδρας γῆς τῆσδ᾽ ἂν ἐξέλθοιμ᾽ ἔτι.

ΞΕΝΟΣ

τί δ᾽ ἐστὶ τοῦτο;

ΟΙΔΙΠΟΥΣ

ξυμφορᾶς ξύνθημ᾽ ἐμῆς.

ΞΕΝΟΣ

ἀλλ᾽ οὐδ᾽ ἐμοί τοι τοὐξανιστάναι πόλεως
δίχ᾽ ἐστὶ θάρσος, πρίν γ᾽ ἂν ἐνδείξω τί δρῶ.

ΟΙΔΙΠΟΥΣ

πρός νυν θεῶν, ὦ ξεῖνε, μή μ᾽ ἀτιμάσῃς,
τοιόνδ᾽ ἀλήτην, ὧν σε προστρέπω φράσαι.

ΞΕΝΟΣ

σήμαινε, κοὐκ ἄτιμος ἔκ γ᾽ ἐμοῦ φανεῖ.

ΟΙΔΙΠΟΥΣ

τίς ἔσθ᾽ ὁ χῶρος δῆτ᾽, ἐν ᾧ βεβήκαμεν;

ΞΕΝΟΣ

ὅσ᾽ οἶδα κἀγὼ πάντ᾽ ἐπιστήσει κλύων·
χῶρος μὲν ἱερὸς πᾶς ὅδ᾽ ἔστ᾽· ἔχει δέ νιν

STRANGER

It's a holy place, where no man may stay—
a sanctuary of goddesses, daughters
of Darkness and of Earth.

OEDIPUS

Tell me their revered names,
so once I hear that I may pray to them.

STRANGER

The people here would call these goddesses
the Eumenides, the all-seeing Kindly Ones.[1]
But elsewhere other names serve just as well.

OEDIPUS

Then I pray they may receive their suppliant
with kindness, for from this sacred refuge,
here in this land, I never will depart.

STRANGER

What do you mean?

OEDIPUS

It has been prearranged—
this is my destiny.[2]

STRANGER

I do not dare
drive you away from here, until I tell
the city what I'm doing and receive
their sanction.

OEDIPUS

By the gods, stranger,
do not dishonour me, a poor wanderer.
I beg you—tell me what I wish to know.

STRANGER

Then speak up. I will not dishonour you.

OEDIPUS

This country we've just reached, what is it called?

STRANGER

Listen. I will tell you everything I know.
This entire place is consecrated ground,

σεμνὸς Ποσειδῶν· ἐν δ' ὁ πυρφόρος θεὸς
Τιτὰν Προμηθεύς· ὃν δ' ἐπιστείβεις τόπον,
χθονὸς καλεῖται τῆσδε χαλκόπους ὀδός,
ἔρεισμ' Ἀθηνῶν· οἱ δὲ πλησίοι γύαι
τόνδ' ἱππότην Κολωνὸν εὔχονται σφίσιν
ἀρχηγὸν εἶναι καὶ φέρουσι τοὔνομα
τὸ τοῦδε κοινὸν πάντες ὠνομασμένοι.
τοιαῦτά σοι ταῦτ' ἐστίν, ὦ ξέν', οὐ λόγοις
τιμώμεν', ἀλλὰ τῇ ξυνουσίᾳ πλέον.

ΟΙΔΙΠΟΥΣ
ἦ γάρ τινες ναίουσι τούσδε τοὺς τόπους;

ΞΕΝΟΣ
καὶ κάρτα, τοῦδε τοῦ θεοῦ γ' ἐπώνυμοι.

ΟΙΔΙΠΟΥΣ
ἄρχει τις αὐτῶν ἢ 'πὶ τῷ πλήθει λόγος;

ΞΕΝΟΣ
ἐκ τοῦ κατ' ἄστυ βασιλέως τάδ' ἄρχεται.

ΟΙΔΙΠΟΥΣ
οὗτος δὲ τίς λόγῳ τε καὶ σθένει κρατεῖ;

ΞΕΝΟΣ
Θησεὺς καλεῖται, τοῦ πρὶν Αἰγέως τόκος.

ΟΙΔΙΠΟΥΣ
ἆρ' ἄν τις αὐτῷ πομπὸς ἐξ ὑμῶν μόλοι;

ΞΕΝΟΣ
ὡς πρὸς τί λέξων ἢ καταρτύσων μολεῖν;

ΟΙΔΙΠΟΥΣ
ὡς ἂν προσαρκῶν σμικρὰ κερδάνῃ μέγα.

ΞΕΝΟΣ
καὶ τίς πρὸς ἀνδρὸς μὴ βλέποντος ἄρκεσις;

owned by divine Poseidon. In it, too,
dwells the Titan god, the fire bearer,
Prometheus.[3] That spot where you now sit
is called this land's bronze threshold, a place
that safeguards Athens.[4] The neighbouring lands
claim horseman Colonus was their ruler
in ancient times, and they all bear his name
in common. That's what these holy places are,
stranger. We do not honour them in story
but rather by living here among them.

OEDIPUS
So this land truly has inhabitants.

STRANGER *[pointing to a statue nearby]*
Indeed it does. And they derive their name
from that hero over there, from Colonus.[5]

OEDIPUS
Who governs them? Do they have a king,
or is there a popular assembly?

STRANGER
The king of Athens rules the people here.

OEDIPUS
What man now speaks and acts with royal power?

STRANGER
His name is Theseus, son of Aegeus,
who was king before him.

OEDIPUS
Is it possible
for one of you to reach him with a message?

STRANGER
With what in mind? To tell him something
or encourage him to come in person?

OEDIPUS
To inform him that a trifling service
will garner him great reward.

STRANGER
What assistance
can a man who does not see provide?

Οιδιπουσ

ὅσ’ ἂν λέγωμεν πάνθ’ ὁρῶντα λέξομεν.

Ξενοσ

οἶσθ’, ὦ ξέν’, ὡς νῦν μὴ σφαλῇς; ἐπείπερ εἶ
γενναῖος, ὡς ἰδόντι, πλὴν τοῦ δαίμονος,
αὐτοῦ μέν’ οὗπερ κἀφάνης, ἕως ἐγὼ
τοῖς ἐνθάδ’ αὐτοῦ μὴ κατ’ ἄστυ δημόταις
λέξω τάδ’ ἐλθών· οἵδε γὰρ κρινοῦσί σοι
εἰ χρή σε μίμνειν ἢ πορεύεσθαι πάλιν.

Οιδιπουσ

ὦ τέκνον, ἦ βέβηκεν ἡμὶν ὁ ξένος;

Αντιγονη

βέβηκεν, ὥστε πᾶν ἐν ἡσύχῳ, πάτερ,
ἔξεστι φωνεῖν, ὡς ἐμοῦ μόνης πέλας.

Οιδιπουσ

ὦ πότνιαι δεινῶπες, εὖτε νῦν ἕδρας
πρώτων ἐφ’ ὑμῶν τῆσδε γῆς ἔκαμψ’ ἐγώ,
Φοίβῳ τε κἀμοὶ μὴ γένησθ’ ἀγνώμονες,
ὅς μοι, τὰ πόλλ’ ἐκεῖν’ ὅτ’ ἐξέχρη κακά,
ταύτην ἔλεξε παῦλαν ἐν χρόνῳ μακρῷ,
ἐλθόντι χώραν τερμίαν, ὅπου θεῶν
σεμνῶν ἕδραν λάβοιμι καὶ ξενόστασιν,
ἐνταῦθα κάμψειν τὸν ταλαίπωρον βίον,
κέρδη μὲν οἰκήσαντα τοῖς δεδεγμένοις,
ἄτην δὲ τοῖς πέμψασιν, οἵ μ’ ἀπήλασαν·
σημεῖα δ’ ἥξειν τῶνδέ μοι παρηγγύα,
ἢ σεισμὸν ἢ βροντήν τιν’ ἢ Διὸς σέλας,
ἔγνωκα μέν νυν ὥς με τήνδε τὴν ὁδὸν
οὐκ ἔσθ’ ὅπως οὐ πιστὸν ἐξ ὑμῶν πτερὸν
ἐξήγαγ’ εἰς τόδ’ ἄλσος· οὐ γὰρ ἄν ποτε

OEDIPUS
The words I say have visionary power.

STRANGER
Be careful, stranger, not to come to grief.
For, quite apart from your unlucky fate,
I see you have a true nobility.
Wait where you are. I am going to go
and tell the people what is happening—
those in this district, not the city folk.
They will determine whether you should stay
or travel back again.

[The STRANGER leaves]

OEDIPUS
Tell me, my child,
has that stranger left us?

ANTIGONE
He has, father.
You are free to say whatever you wish.
I am the only person close to you.

OEDIPUS
O you fierce-eyed, reverend divinities,
since here at Athens it was at your shrine
I first sought refuge, may you not be ungracious
to Phoebus and to me. When he prophesied
the many evils I would undergo,
he said eventually I would find rest,
once I reached my final goal in a place
where I would find a sacred sanctuary
of dreadful goddesses, shelter for strangers,
and there my life of suffering would end.
By remaining in that land I would bring
advantages to those who welcomed me
and ruin to the ones who drove me out,
who exiled me from Thebes. Apollo said
that signs of this would come to me—earthquakes
and thunder or a lightning flash from Zeus.
I now recognize it surely must have been
some trusty omen sent from you that led me
on my journey to this consecrated ground.

πρώταισιν ὑμῖν ἀντέκυρσ' ὁδοιπορῶν,
νήφων ἀοίνοις, κἀπὶ σεμνὸν ἑζόμην
βάθρον τόδ' ἀσκέπαρνον. ἀλλά μοι, θεαί,
βίου κατ' ὀμφὰς τὰς Ἀπόλλωνος δότε
πέρασιν ἤδη καὶ καταστροφήν τινα,
εἰ μὴ δοκῶ τι μειόνως ἔχειν, ἀεὶ
μόχθοις λατρεύων τοῖς ὑπερτάτοις βροτῶν.
ἴτ', ὦ γλυκεῖαι παῖδες ἀρχαίου Σκότου,
ἴτ', ὦ μεγίστης Παλλάδος καλούμεναι
πασῶν Ἀθῆναι τιμιωτάτη πόλις,
οἰκτίρατ' ἀνδρὸς Οἰδίπου τόδ' ἄθλιον
εἴδωλον· οὐ γὰρ δὴ τόδ' ἀρχαῖον δέμας.

ΑΝΤΙΓΟΝΗ

σίγα· πορεύονται γὰρ οἵδε δή τινες
χρόνῳ παλαιοί, σῆς ἕδρας ἐπίσκοποι.

ΟΙΔΙΠΟΥΣ

σιγήσομαί τε καὶ σύ μ' ἐξ ὁδοῦ πόδα
κρύψον κατ' ἄλσος, τῶνδ' ἕως ἂν ἐκμάθω
τίνας λόγους ἐροῦσιν· ἐν γὰρ τῷ μαθεῖν
ἔνεστιν ηὑλάβεια τῶν ποιουμένων.

ΧΟΡΟΣ

ὅρα. τίς ἄρ' ἦν; ποῦ ναίει;
ποῦ κυρεῖ ἐκτόπιος συθεὶς ὁ πάντων
ὁ πάντων ἀκορέστατος;
προσδέρκου λεῦσσέ νιν,
προσπεύθου πανταχῇ.
πλανάτας πλανάτας τις ὁ πρέσβυς οὐδ'
ἔγχωρος· προσέβα γὰρ οὐκ
ἄν ποτ' ἀστιβὲς ἄλσος ἐς
τᾶνδ' ἀμαιμακετᾶν κορᾶν,
ἃς τρέμομεν λέγειν
καὶ παραμειβόμεσθ' ἀδέρκτως,

How otherwise, in my wandering around,
would I, a temperate man, first have met
you austere goddesses, who touch no wine,
or sat down on this sacred rough-hewn rock.[6]
O you deities, I pray you let me
follow what Apollo's oracle decreed
and end my life at last, unless perhaps
I seem unworthy, enslaved to misery
far worse than any other mortal man.[7]
Hear me, sweet daughters of eternal Darkness!
Hear me, city named for mighty Pallas,
O Athens, most honoured of all cities,
pity the poor ghost of that man Oedipus,
for now his old living body is no more.

ANTIGONE

You should stop talking. Some old men are coming
to check out the place where you are sitting.

OEDIPUS

I will be quiet. Hide me in the grove
some distance from the road, until I learn
what these men are saying. That is something
we must find out in order to act safely.

[ANTIGONE leads OEDIPUS to a hiding place. Enter the CHORUS, elderly citizens of Colonus]

CHORUS

Look around. Who was that man,
that most presumptuous of mortals?
Where did he go when he left here?
Keep a sharp look out. Search the place.
Hunt everywhere. That old man
must be a wandering vagabond,
and not a local citizen,
for otherwise he'd never dare
to set foot in the sacred grove
dedicated to those goddesses
no one can resist—whose very names
we cannot utter without trembling,
and from whose gaze when we walk past
we avert our eyes and look away,

ἀφώνως, ἀλόγως τὸ τᾶς.
εὐφάμου στόμα φροντίδος
ἱέντες, τὰ δὲ νῦν τιν' ἥκειν
λόγος οὐδὲν ἅζονθ',
ὃν ἐγὼ λεύσσων περὶ πᾶν οὔπω
δύναμαι τέμενος
γνῶναι ποῦ μοί ποτε ναίει.

ΟΙΔΙΠΟΥΣ
ὅδ' ἐκεῖνος ἐγώ· φωνῇ γὰρ ὁρῶ,
τὸ φατιζόμενον.

ΧΟΡΟΣ
ἰὼ ἰώ,
δεινὸς μὲν ὁρᾶν, δεινὸς δὲ κλύειν.

ΟΙΔΙΠΟΥΣ
μή μ', ἱκετεύω, προσίδητ' ἄνομον.

ΧΟΡΟΣ
Ζεῦ ἀλεξῆτορ, τίς ποθ' ὁ πρέσβυς;

ΟΙΔΙΠΟΥΣ
οὐ πάνυ μοίρας εὐδαιμονίσαι
πρώτης, ὦ τῆσδ' ἔφοροι χώρας.
δηλῶ δ'· οὐ γὰρ ἂν ὧδ' ἀλλοτρίοις
ὄμμασιν εἷρπον
κἀπὶ σμικροῖς μέγας ὥρμουν.

ΧΟΡΟΣ
ἐή, ἀλαῶν ὀμμάτων
ἆρα καὶ ἦσθα φυτάλμιος; δυσαίων
μακραίων γ', ὅσ' ἐπεικάσαι.
ἀλλ' οὐ μὰν ἔν γ' ἐμοὶ
προσθήσει τάσδ' ἀράς.
περᾷς γάρ, περᾷς· ἀλλ' ἵνα τῷδ' ἐν ἀ-
φθέγκτῳ μὴ προπέσῃς νάπει
ποιάεντι, κάθυδρος οὗ

without a word, our voices mute,
mouthing pious thoughts in silence.
Now, so they say, someone has come,
who has no reverence for these deities.
We've searched this sacred shrine
and caught no glimpse of him.
I do not know where he is hiding.

[OEDIPUS and ANTIGONE leave their hiding place and move forward]

OEDIPUS
I am the one you seek. The sounds you make
serve me instead of sight, as people say
of men who cannot see.

CHORUS *[horrified]*
Aaaiii, Aaaiii!
What a horrific sight! And that fearful voice!

OEDIPUS
Do not consider me outside the law—
I'm begging you!

CHORUS
By our defender Zeus,
who could this old man be?

OEDIPUS
You citizens,
guardians of this land, I am a man whose fate
no one could call happy. That much is clear,
for otherwise I would not creep around
requiring help from someone else's eyes,
my great age propped up by this weak young girl.

CHORUS
Ah, have you been blind since you were born?
It looks as if a long and wretched life
has been your lot. But if I can stop you,
in this place you will bring no more curses
down on yourself. You go too far—too far!
O you most wretched of all strangers,
do not stumble into this grassy shrine
where no one is allowed to speak,

κρατὴρ μειλιχίων ποτῶν
ῥεύματι συντρέχει,
τόν, ξένε πάμμορ', εὖ φύλαξαι;
μετάσταθ' ἀπόβαθι. πολ-
λὰ κέλευθος ἐρατύει·
κλύεις, ὦ πολύμοχθ' ἀλᾶτα;
λόγον εἴ τιν' οἴσεις
πρὸς ἐμὰν λέσχαν, ἀβάτων ἀποβάς,
ἵνα πᾶσι νόμος,
φώνει· πρόσθεν δ' ἀπερύκου.

ΟΙΔΙΠΟΥΣ

θύγατερ, ποῖ τις φροντίδος ἔλθῃ;

ΑΝΤΙΓΟΝΗ

ὦ πάτερ, ἀστοῖς ἴσα χρὴ μελετᾶν,
εἴκοντας ἃ δεῖ κἀκούοντας.

ΟΙΔΙΠΟΥΣ

πρόσθιγέ νύν μου.

ΑΝΤΙΓΟΝΗ

ψαύω καὶ δή.

ΟΙΔΙΠΟΥΣ

ὦ ξένε, μὴ δῆτ' ἀδικηθῶ σοὶ
πιστεύσας καὶ μεταναστάς.

ΧΟΡΟΣ

οὔ τοι μήποτέ σ' ἐκ τῶνδ' ἑδράνων,
ὦ γέρον, ἄκοντά τις ἄξει.

ΟΙΔΙΠΟΥΣ

ἔτ' οὖν;

ΧΟΡΟΣ

ἔτι βαῖνε πόρσω.

ΟΙΔΙΠΟΥΣ

ἔτι;

where honey offerings and sweet water
pour from the mixing bowl.[8]
I am giving you fair warning.
Move back from there. Withdraw,
and keep your distance. You hear me,
you long-suffering wanderer?
If you have anything to say to us,
leave that forbidden ground.
Talk where people are allowed to speak.
Until that time, be silent.

OEDIPUS
Daughter, what course of action should we choose?

ANTIGONE
We must obey the customs here, father,
act as the locals do. We must listen
and where we have no choice do what they say.

OEDIPUS
Then take my hand.

ANTIGONE
I have it.

OEDIPUS
Strangers,
if I trust you and leave this sanctuary,
do not harm me.

CHORUS
Old man, no one will ever
take you from your refuge here against your will.

[OEDIPUS starts to move out of his hiding place]

OEDIPUS
Is this far enough?

CHORUS
Move on a little more.

OEDIPUS
Further still?

Χορος

προβίβαζε, κούρα,
πόρσω· σὺ γὰρ ἀΐεις.

Αντιγονη

<. . .>

Οιδιπους

<. . .>

Αντιγονη

<. . .>
ἕπεο μάν, ἕπε᾽ ὧδ᾽ ἀμαυρῷ
κώλῳ, πάτερ, σ᾽ ἄγω.

Χορος

τόλμα ξεῖνος ἐπὶ ξένης,
ὦ τλάμων, ὅ τι καὶ πόλις
τέτροφεν ἄφιλον ἀποστυγεῖν
καὶ τὸ φίλον σέβεσθαι.

Οιδιπους

ἄγε νυν σύ με, παῖ,
ἵν᾽ ἂν εὐσεβίας ἐπιβαίνοντες
τὸ μὲν εἴποιμεν, τὸ δ᾽ ἀκούσαιμεν,
καὶ μὴ χρείᾳ πολεμῶμεν.

Χορος

αὐτοῦ· μηκέτι τοῦδ᾽ αὐτοπέτρου
βήματος ἔξω πόδα κλίνῃς.

Οιδιπους

οὕτως;

Χορος

ἅλις, ὡς ἀκούεις.

Οιδιπους

ἦ ἐσθῶ;

CHORUS

You know what me mean, young girl—
lead him out this way.

[..][9]

ANTIGONE

Come, father, let your dark steps follow me.
I'll lead you out.

CHORUS

Stranger in a foreign land,
you ill-fated man, you must have courage
to hate what the city here has grown to hate
and to love what it holds dear.

OEDIPUS

Lead me out,
my child, to where we may speak and listen,
treading a path of pious righteousness,
not waging war against necessity.

CHORUS

There! Do not step beyond that rocky ledge!

OEDIPUS

Right here?

CHORUS

That's far enough. Are you listening?

OEDIPUS

Should I sit down?

ΧΟΡΟΣ

λέχριός γ' ἐπ' ἄκρου
λᾶος βραχὺς ὀκλάσας.

ΑΝΤΙΓΟΝΗ

πάτερ, ἐμὸν τόδ'· ἐν ἁσυχαίᾳ

ΟΙΔΙΠΟΥΣ

ἰώ μοί μοι.

ΑΝΤΙΓΟΝΗ

βάσει βάσιν ἅρμοσαι,
γεραὸν ἐς χέρα σῶμα σὸν
προκλίνας φιλίαν ἐμάν.

ΟΙΔΙΠΟΥΣ

ὤμοι δύσφρονος ἄτας.

ΧΟΡΟΣ

ὦ τλάμων, ὅτε νῦν χαλᾷς,
αὔδασον, τίς ἔφυς βροτῶν;
τίς ὁ πολύπονος ἄγει; τίν' ἂν
σοῦ πατρίδ' ἐκπυθοίμαν;

ΟΙΔΙΠΟΥΣ

ὦ ξένοι, ἀπόπτολις· ἀλλὰ μὴ

ΧΟΡΟΣ

τί τόδ' ἀπεννέπεις, γέρον;

ΟΙΔΙΠΟΥΣ

μὴ μὴ μή μ' ἀνέρῃ τίς εἰμι, μηδ' ἐξετάσῃς πέρα
ματεύων.

ΧΟΡΟΣ

τί τόδ';

ΟΙΔΙΠΟΥΣ

αἰνὰ φύσις.

CHORUS

Move sideways and crouch there—
down on the edge of that low rock.

ANTIGONE

Father,
let me do it. Gently now . . .

OEDIPUS

Alas for me!

ANTIGONE *[helping OEDIPUS sit down]*

. . . match me step for step. Lean your ancient frame
here on my loving arm.

Oedipus

Ah, my dreadful fate!

CHORUS

Now you are seated, you unfortunate man,
speak to us. From what line of mortal men
do you descend? Who are you to be led like this
in such distress? What land do you call home?

OEDIPUS

Strangers, I am a man who has been banished.
I have no home. But do not . . .

CHORUS

What is it, old man,
you would not have us do?

OEDIPUS

You must not ask . . .
you must not ask me who I am.

CHORUS

Why not?

OEDIPUS

My origin is dreadful.

ΧΟΡΟΣ

αὔδα.

ΟΙΔΙΠΟΥΣ

τέκνον, ὤμοι, τί γεγώνω;

ΧΟΡΟΣ

τίνος εἶ σπέρματος, ὦ ξένε, φώνει, πατρόθεν.

ΟΙΔΙΠΟΥΣ

ὤμοι ἐγώ, τί πάθω, τέκνον ἐμόν;

ΑΝΤΙΓΟΝΗ

λέγ᾽, ἐπείπερ ἐπ᾽ ἔσχατα βαίνεις.

ΟΙΔΙΠΟΥΣ

ἀλλ᾽ ἐρῶ· οὐ γὰρ ἔχω κατακρυφάν.

ΧΟΡΟΣ

μακρὰ μέλλετον, ἀλλὰ τάχυνε.

ΟΙΔΙΠΟΥΣ

Λαΐου ἴστε τιν᾽;

ΧΟΡΟΣ

ὢ ἰοὺ ἰού.

ΟΙΔΙΠΟΥΣ

τό τε Λαβδακιδᾶν γένος;

ΧΟΡΟΣ

ὦ Ζεῦ.

ΟΙΔΙΠΟΥΣ

ἄθλιον Οἰδιπόδαν;

ΧΟΡΟΣ

σὺ γὰρ ὅδ᾽ εἶ;

ΟΙΔΙΠΟΥΣ

δέος ἴσχετε μηδὲν ὅσ᾽ αὐδῶ.

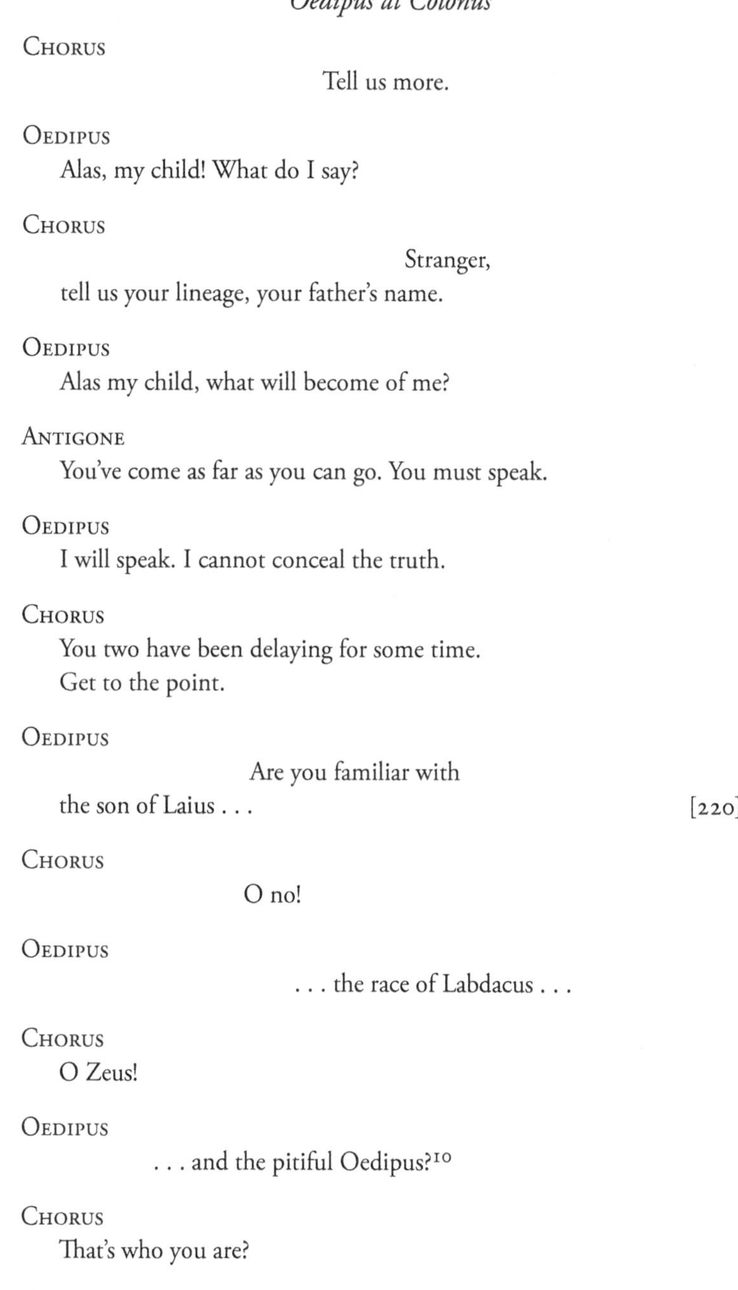

CHORUS

Tell us more.

OEDIPUS

Alas, my child! What do I say?

CHORUS

Stranger,
tell us your lineage, your father's name.

OEDIPUS

Alas my child, what will become of me?

ANTIGONE

You've come as far as you can go. You must speak.

OEDIPUS

I will speak. I cannot conceal the truth.

CHORUS

You two have been delaying for some time.
Get to the point.

OEDIPUS

Are you familiar with
the son of Laius . . .

CHORUS

O no!

OEDIPUS

. . . the race of Labdacus . . .

CHORUS

O Zeus!

OEDIPUS

. . . and the pitiful Oedipus?[10]

CHORUS

That's who you are?

OEDIPUS

You must not be afraid
of anything I say.

Χορος

ἰὼ ὢ ὤ.

Οιδιπους

δύσμορος.

Χορος

ὢ ὤ.

Οιδιπους

θύγατερ, τί ποτ᾽ αὐτίκα κύρσει;

Χορος

ἔξω πόρσω βαίνετε χώρας.

Οιδιπους

ἃ δ᾽ ὑπέσχεο ποῖ καταθήσεις,

Χορος

οὐδενὶ μοιριδία τίσις ἔρχεται
ὧν προπάθῃ τὸ τίνειν·
ἀπάτα δ᾽ ἀπάταις ἑτέραις ἑτέρα
παραβαλλομένα πόνον, οὐ χάριν, ἀντιδίδωσιν ἔχειν.
σὺ δὲ τῶνδ᾽ ἑδράνων πάλιν ἔκτοπος αὖθις ἄφορμος ἐμᾶς
χθονὸς ἔκθορε, μή τι πέρα χρέος
ἐμᾷ πόλει προσάψῃς.

Αντιγονη

ὦ ξένοι αἰδόφρονες,
ἀλλ᾽ ἐπεὶ γεραὸν πατέρα
τόνδ᾽ ἐμὸν οὐκ ἀνέτλατ᾽, ἔργων
ἀκόντων ἀΐοντες αὐδάν,
ἀλλ᾽ ἐμὲ τὰν μελέαν, ἱκετεύομεν,
ὦ ξένοι, οἰκτίραθ᾽, ἃ
πατρὸς ὑπὲρ τοὐμοῦ μόνου
ἄντομαι οὐκ ἀλαοῖς προσορωμένα
ὄμμα σὸν ὄμμασιν, ὥς τις ἀφ᾽ αἵματος
ὑμετέρου προφανεῖσα, τὸν ἄθλιον
αἰδοῦς κῦρσαι· ἐν ὔμμι γὰρ ὡς θεῷ
κείμεθα τλάμονες. ἀλλ᾽ ἴτε, νεύσατε
τὰν ἀδόκητον χάριν·

Chorus

O no! No! No!

Oedipus

I am so wretched!

Chorus

No! No!

Oedipus

My daughter,

what will happen now?

Chorus

You must leave this land.

Go away!

Oedipus

What about those words you swore?
How will you keep your promises to me?[11]

Chorus

A man incurs no punishment from Fate
when he responds to evils done to him.
You deceived us—now we are doing the same.
Such actions bring no gratifying reward
but merely pain.[12] So you must go away,
leave where you are sitting, set off again,
and hurry out of Athens without delay,
in case you bring pollution to our state.

Antigone

You reverend strangers, you do not accept
my aged father. You have heard the stories
and know what he did without intending to.
But, strangers, at least pity me, a poor girl,
I beg you, as I plead for him alone,
my father. I implore you with these eyes,
which can still gaze into your own, like one
who shares your blood, let this suffering man
win your compassion. In our wretched state
you are like gods—we are in your power.
Grant us this unexpected benefit!

πρός σ᾽ ὅ τι σοι φίλον ἐκ σέθεν ἄντομαι,
ἢ τέκνον ἢ λέχος ἢ χρέος ἢ θεός·
οὐ γὰρ ἴδοις ἂν ἀθρῶν βροτὸν
ὅστις ἄν, εἰ θεὸς ἄγοι,
ἐκφυγεῖν δύναιτο.

Χορος

ἀλλ᾽ ἴσθι, τέκνον Οἰδίπου, σέ τ᾽ ἐξ ἴσου
οἰκτίρομεν καὶ τόνδε συμφορᾶς χάριν·
τὰ δ᾽ ἐκ θεῶν τρέμοντες οὐ σθένοιμεν ἂν
φωνεῖν πέρα τῶν πρὸς σὲ νῦν εἰρημένων.

Οιδιπους

τί δῆτα δόξης ἢ τί κληδόνος καλῆς
μάτην ῥεούσης ὠφέλημα γίγνεται,
εἰ τάς γ᾽ Ἀθήνας φασὶ θεοσεβεστάτας
εἶναι, μόνας δὲ τὸν κακούμενον ξένον
σῴζειν οἵας τε καὶ μόνας ἀρκεῖν ἔχειν;
κἄμοιγε ποῦ τοῦτ᾽ ἐστίν, οἵτινες βάθρων
ἐκ τῶνδέ μ᾽ ἐξάραντες εἶτ᾽ ἐλαύνετε,
ὄνομα μόνον δείσαντες; οὐ γὰρ δὴ τό γε
σῶμ᾽ οὐδὲ τἄργα τἄμ᾽· ἐπεὶ τά γ᾽ ἔργα μου
πεπονθότ᾽ ἐστὶ μᾶλλον ἢ δεδρακότα,
εἴ σοι τὰ μητρὸς καὶ πατρὸς χρείη λέγειν,
ὧν οὕνεκ᾽ ἐκφοβεῖ με· τοῦτ᾽ ἐγὼ καλῶς
ἔξοιδα. καίτοι πῶς ἐγὼ κακὸς φύσιν,
ὅστις παθὼν μὲν ἀντέδρων, ὥστ᾽ εἰ φρονῶν
ἔπρασσον, οὐδ᾽ ἂν ὧδ᾽ ἐγιγνόμην κακός;
νῦν δ᾽ οὐδὲν εἰδὼς ἱκόμην ἵν᾽ ἱκόμην,
ὑφ᾽ ὧν δ᾽ ἔπασχον, εἰδότων ἀπωλλύμην.
ἀνθ᾽ ὧν ἱκνοῦμαι πρὸς θεῶν ὑμᾶς, ξένοι,
ὥσπερ με κἀνεστήσαθ᾽, ὧδε σώσατε,
καὶ μὴ θεοὺς τιμῶντες εἶτα τοὺς θεοὺς
μοίρας ποιεῖσθε μηδαμῶς· ἡγεῖσθε δὲ

I'm begging you by all the things you love,
your child, your wife, your property, your gods!
No matter where you search, you will not find
a mortal man who can escape the gods
when they lead him to disaster.

CHORUS

Know this,
child of Oedipus, we do have pity
for you and him alike in your ordeal.
But we fear what the gods may do to us
and lack the power to say anything
other than what we have said already.

OEDIPUS

What use is a fine reputation then
or glory, if what it turns out to be
is empty breath? People claim that Athens,
more than any other place, reveres the gods
and is the only city with the strength
to save a stranger in distress—it alone
can rescue him. Yet in my situation
where are these qualities? You have made me
rise from that rock ledge and will drive me out
only because my name makes you afraid.
For surely you cannot fear my presence
or my actions, because, if I must tell
the story of my father and my mother—
which is why you fear me—then what matters
is not what I did but what I suffered.
I know that well. So how am I by birth
an evil man, when I was reacting
to others who had harmed me? Even if
I had fully known what I was doing,
you would not allege that I was evil.[13]
But as it was, when I went where I did
I knew nothing, while those who injured me
in full knowledge of what they were doing
sought my destruction.[14] And therefore, strangers,
I'm begging you, in the name of the gods,
just as you made me leave my refuge,
rescue me. While you pay tribute to the gods,
do not, at any moment, act impiously.

βλέπειν μὲν αὐτοὺς πρὸς τὸν εὐσεβῆ βροτῶν,
βλέπειν δὲ πρὸς τοὺς δυσσεβεῖς, φυγὴν δέ του
μήπω γενέσθαι φωτὸς ἀνοσίου βροτῶν.
ξὺν οἷς σὺ μὴ κάλυπτε τὰς εὐδαίμονας
ἔργοις Ἀθήνας ἀνοσίοις ὑπηρετῶν,
ἀλλ' ὥσπερ ἔλαβες τὸν ἱκέτην ἐχέγγυον,
ῥύου με κἀκφύλασσε· μηδέ μου κάρα
τὸ δυσπρόσοπτον εἰσορῶν ἀτιμάσῃς,
ἥκω γὰρ ἱερὸς εὐσεβής τε καὶ φέρων
ὄνησιν ἀστοῖς τοῖσδ'· ὅταν δ' ὁ κύριος
παρῇ τις, ὑμῶν ὅστις ἐστὶν ἡγεμών,
τότ' εἰσακούων πάντ' ἐπιστήσει· τὰ δὲ
μεταξὺ τούτου μηδαμῶς γίγνου κακός.

Χορος

ταρβεῖν μέν, ὦ γεραιέ, τἀνθυμήματα
πολλή 'στ' ἀνάγκη τἀπὸ σοῦ· λόγοισι γὰρ
οὐκ ὠνόμασται βραχέσι· τοὺς δὲ τῆσδε γῆς
ἄνακτας ἀρκεῖ ταῦτά μοι διειδέναι.

Οιδιπους

καὶ ποῦ 'σθ' ὁ κραίνων τῆσδε τῆς χώρας, ξένοι;

Χορος

πατρῷον ἄστυ γῆς ἔχει· σκοπὸς δέ νιν,
ὃς κἀμὲ δεῦρ' ἔπεμψεν, οἴχεται στελῶν.

Οιδιπους

ἦ καὶ δοκεῖτε τοῦ τυφλοῦ τιν' ἐντροπὴν
ἢ φροντίδ', ἕξειν, αὐτὸν ὥστ' ἐλθεῖν πέλας;

Χορος

καὶ κάρθ', ὅταν περ τοὔνομ' αἴσθηται τὸ σόν.

Οιδιπους

τίς δ' ἔσθ' ὁ κείνῳ τοῦτο τοὔπος ἀγγελῶν;

Χορος

μακρὰ κέλευθος· πολλὰ δ' ἐμπόρων ἔπη

Consider this: they watch those who believe
as well as those who show them no respect,
and never yet has any godless man
escaped them. Strangers, seek help from the gods,
and do not shame the good name of Athens
by lowering yourselves to profane deeds.
You have given this suppliant your pledge,
so take me in, protect me to the end.
This face of mine is horrible to look at,
but when you do, do not dishonour me,
for I have come, a pious, holy man,
bringing benefits to all the citizens.
Once your ruler comes, whoever he is
who is your leader, he will hear all things
and understand. Meanwhile, do not harm me.

CHORUS

The argument you have just made, old man,
in words that carry weight, we must respect.
In my view this issue must be resolved
by those who rule this land.

OEDIPUS

And where, strangers,
is the ruler of this state?

CHORUS

In the city
of his ancestors, here in this land. The scout
who sent us out has gone to summon him.

OEDIPUS

Do you think he will be concerned enough
about a blind man to come in person?

CHORUS

Of course he will, once he finds out your name.

OEDIPUS

Who will tell him that?

CHORUS

It's a long distance,
and many things that travellers report

φιλεῖ πλανᾶσθαι, τῶν ἐκεῖνος ἀΐων,
θάρσει, παρέσται. πολὺ γάρ, ὦ γέρον, τὸ σὸν
ὄνομα διήκει πάντας, ὥστε κεἰ βραδὺς
εὕδει, κλύων σοῦ δεῦρ' ἀφίξεται ταχύς.

ΟΙΔΙΠΟΥΣ

ἀλλ' εὐτυχὴς ἵκοιτο τῇ θ' αὑτοῦ πόλει
ἐμοί τε· τίς γὰρ ἐσθλὸς οὐχ αὑτῷ φίλος;

ΑΝΤΙΓΟΝΗ

ὦ Ζεῦ, τί λέξω; ποῖ φρενῶν ἔλθω, πάτερ;

ΟΙΔΙΠΟΥΣ

τί δ' ἔστι, τέκνον Ἀντιγόνη;

ΑΝΤΙΓΟΝΗ

γυναῖχ' ὁρῶ
στείχουσαν ἡμῶν ἆσσον, Αἰτναίας ἐπὶ
πώλου βεβῶσαν· κρατὶ δ' ἡλιοστεγὴς
κυνῆ πρόσωπα Θεσσαλίς νιν ἀμπέχει.
τί φῶ;
ἆρ' ἔστιν; ἆρ' οὐκ ἔστιν; ἢ γνώμη πλανᾷ;
καὶ φημὶ κἀπόφημι κοὐκ ἔχω τί φῶ.
τάλαινα.
οὐκ ἔστιν ἄλλη· φαιδρὰ γοῦν ἀπ' ὀμμάτων
σαίνει με προσστείχουσα· σημαίνει δ' ὅτι
μόνης τόδ' ἐστὶ δῆλον Ἰσμήνης κάρα.

ΟΙΔΙΠΟΥΣ

πῶς εἶπας, ὦ παῖ;

ΑΝΤΙΓΟΝΗ

παῖδα σήν, ἐμὴν δ' ὁρᾶν
ὅμαιμον· αὐδῇ δ' αὐτίκ' ἔξεστιν μαθεῖν.

get passed around. There is no need to worry.
Once he hears the news, he will come to us.
We are all familiar with your name, old man,
so even if the king is tired and resting,
when he learns of you he'll soon be here.

OEDIPUS

May he get here quickly and bring good fortune
to me and to his city. What decent man
does not help himself by helping others?

ANTIGONE

O Zeus! What am I going to say, father?
What should I think?

OEDIPUS

Antigone my child,
what is it?

ANTIGONE

I see a woman coming here
riding a pony—a young Sicilian horse.
She's wearing a Thessalian cloth hat
to keep her face protected from the sun.
What am I to say? Is it her or not?
My mind keeps changing! Should I say it's her
or someone else? What a wretched business!
Yes, it must be her. As she gets closer,
the brightness in her eyes is welcoming me.
She's giving me a signal! It's obvious—
the rider has to be Ismene.

OEDIPUS

My child,
what are you saying?

ANTIGONE

I see my sister,
your daughter! You'll recognize her soon enough,
once you hear her voice.

[Enter ISMENE][15]

ΙΣΜΗΝΗ

ὦ δισσὰ πατρὸς καὶ κασιγνήτης ἐμοὶ
ἥδιστα προσφωνήμαθ', ὡς ὑμᾶς μόλις
εὑροῦσα λύπῃ δεύτερον μόλις βλέπω.

ΟΙΔΙΠΟΥΣ

ὦ τέκνον, ἥκεις;

ΙΣΜΗΝΗ

ὦ πάτερ δύσμοιρ' ὁρᾶν.

ΟΙΔΙΠΟΥΣ

τέκνον, πέφηνας;

ΙΣΜΗΝΗ

οὐκ ἄνευ μόχθου γέ μοι.

ΟΙΔΙΠΟΥΣ

πρόσψαυσον, ὦ παῖ.

ΙΣΜΗΝΗ

θιγγάνω δυοῖν ὁμοῦ.

ΟΙΔΙΠΟΥΣ

ὦ σπέρμ' ὅμαιμον.

ΙΣΜΗΝΗ

ὦ δυσάθλιαι τροφαί.

ΟΙΔΙΠΟΥΣ

ἦ τῆσδε κἀμοῦ;

ΙΣΜΗΝΗ

δυσμόρου τ' ἐμοῦ τρίτης.

ΟΙΔΙΠΟΥΣ

τέκνον, τί δ' ἦλθες;

ΙΣΜΗΝΗ

σῇ, πάτερ, προμηθίᾳ.

ISMENE

Ah, there you are, you two,
my father and my sister, a double joy
to utter those two words. How difficult
it was to find you—and now how painful
it is to look at you!

OEDIPUS

Are you here, my child?

ISMENE

O father, your fate is sad to witness!

OEDIPUS

O Ismene, have you really come?

ISMENE

Yes I have.
But travelling here was not easy for me.

OEDIPUS

Touch me, my child.

ISMENE

I'll hold you both at once.

OEDIPUS

O children of my blood!

ISMENE

What wretched lives!

OEDIPUS

Antigone's and mine?

ISMENE

And mine as well.
I am the third whose life is miserable.

OEDIPUS

Child, why have you come?

ISMENE

I came for your sake—
I'm concerned about you.

ΟΙΔΙΠΟΥΣ

πότερα πόθοισι;

ΙΣΜΗΝΗ

καὶ λόγων γ' αὐτάγγελος,
ξὺν ᾧπερ εἶχον οἰκετῶν πιστῷ μόνῳ.

ΟΙΔΙΠΟΥΣ

οἱ δ' αὐθόμαιμοι ποῦ νεανίαι πονεῖν;

ΙΣΜΗΝΗ

εἴσ' οὗπέρ εἰσι· δεινὰ τἀν κείνοις τανῦν.

ΟΙΔΙΠΟΥΣ

ὦ πάντ' ἐκείνω τοῖς ἐν Αἰγύπτῳ νόμοις
φύσιν κατεικασθέντε καὶ βίου τροφάς·
ἐκεῖ γὰρ οἱ μὲν ἄρσενες κατὰ στέγας
θακοῦσιν ἱστουργοῦντες, αἱ δὲ σύννομοι
τἄξω βίου τροφεῖα πορσύνουσ' ἀεί.
σφῷν δ', ὦ τέκν', οὓς μὲν εἰκὸς ἦν πονεῖν τάδε,
κατ' οἶκον οἰκουροῦσιν ὥστε παρθένοι,
σφὼ δ' ἀντ' ἐκείνων τἀμὰ δυστήνου κακὰ
ὑπερπονεῖτον. ἡ μὲν ἐξ ὅτου νέας
τροφῆς ἔληξε καὶ κατίσχυσεν δέμας,
ἀεὶ μεθ' ἡμῶν δύσμορος πλανωμένη
γερονταγωγεῖ, πολλὰ μὲν κατ' ἀγρίαν
ὕλην ἄσιτος νηλίπους τ' ἀλωμένη,
πολλοῖσι δ' ὄμβροις ἡλίου τε καύμασιν
μοχθοῦσα τλήμων δεύτερ' ἡγεῖται τὰ τῆς
οἴκοι διαίτης, εἰ πατὴρ τροφὴν ἔχοι.
σὺ δ', ὦ τέκνον, πρόσθεν μὲν ἐξίκου πατρὶ
μαντεῖ' ἄγουσα πάντα, Καδμείων λάθρᾳ,
ἃ τοῦδ' ἐχρήσθη σώματος, φύλαξ τέ μου
πιστὴ κατέστης, γῆς ὅτ' ἐξηλαυνόμην·
νῦν δ' αὖ τίν' ἥκεις μῦθον, Ἰσμήνη, πατρὶ
φέρουσα; τίς σ' ἐξῆρεν οἴκοθεν στόλος;
ἥκεις γὰρ οὐ κενή γε, τοῦτ' ἐγὼ σαφῶς
ἔξοιδα, μὴ οὐχὶ δεῖμ' ἐμοὶ φέρουσά τι.

OEDIPUS

Did you miss me?

ISMENE

Yes . . . and I came in person to bring news
with the only trusty servant I possess.

OEDIPUS

Where are your young brothers? They should help you.

ISMENE

They are where they are. Their situation
at the present time is dreadful.

OEDIPUS

Those two!
In their style of life and dispositions,
they always seem to like Egyptian ways,
for in that land men sit around the house
working the loom, while women leave the home
all the time to bring back what they live on.
And in your case, my daughters, those two sons,
who should be doing the work, remain at home,
like girls, while you two assume the burden
of your poor father's pain, instead of them.
This one here, since she stopped being a child
and had sufficient strength, has constantly
been an old man's guide on his harsh journeys,
often wandering barefoot and famished
through savage woods and often beaten down
by storms or the sun's unrelenting heat.
She resolutely sets aside the comforts
home provides, so her father can have food.
And you too, my child, in earlier days,
without the knowledge of those men in Thebes,
came to your father, bringing him reports
of all the oracles concerning Oedipus.
When I was exiled, driven from that land,
you became a faithful sentry for me.
And now here you are again, Ismene.
What recent news have you brought your father?
Why have you made this journey from your home?
You've not come empty handed—that I know—
not without bringing me some new concern.

ΙΣΜΗΝΗ

ἐγὼ τὰ μὲν παθήμαθ᾽ ἅπαθον, πάτερ,
ζητοῦσα τὴν σὴν ποῦ κατοικοίης τροφήν,
παρεῖσ᾽ ἐάσω· δὶς γὰρ οὐχὶ βούλομαι
πονοῦσά τ᾽ ἀλγεῖν καὶ λέγουσ᾽ αὖθις πάλιν.
ἃ δ᾽ ἀμφὶ τοῖν σοῖν δυσμόροιν παίδοιν κακὰ
νῦν ἐστι, ταῦτα σημανοῦσ᾽ ἐλήλυθα.
πρὶν μὲν γὰρ αὐτοῖς ἦν ἔρως Κρέοντί τε
θρόνους ἐᾶσθαι μηδὲ χραίνεσθαι πόλιν,
λόγῳ σκοποῦσι τὴν πάλαι γένους φθοράν,
οἵα κατέσχε τὸν σὸν ἄθλιον δόμον·
νῦν δ᾽ ἐκ θεῶν του κἀλιτηρίου φρενὸς
εἰσῆλθε τοῖν τρὶς ἀθλίοιν ἔρις κακή,
ἀρχῆς λαβέσθαι καὶ κράτους τυραννικοῦ.
χὼ μὲν νεάζων καὶ χρόνῳ μείων γεγὼς
τὸν πρόσθε γεννηθέντα Πολυνείκη θρόνων
ἀποστερίσκει, κἀξελήλακεν πάτρας.
ὁ δ᾽, ὡς καθ᾽ ἡμᾶς ἔσθ᾽ ὁ πληθύων λόγος,
τὸ κοῖλον Ἄργος βὰς φυγὰς προσλαμβάνει
κῆδός τε καινὸν καὶ ξυνασπιστὰς φίλους
ὡς αὐτίκ᾽ Ἄργος ἢ τὸ Καδμείων πέδον
τιμῇ καθέξον ἢ πρὸς οὐρανὸν βιβῶν.
ταῦτ᾽ οὐκ ἀριθμός ἐστιν, ὦ πάτερ, λόγων,
ἀλλ᾽ ἔργα δεινά· τοὺς δὲ σοὺς ὅπου θεοὶ
πόνους κατοικτιοῦσιν οὐκ ἔχω μαθεῖν.

ΟΙΔΙΠΟΥΣ

ἤδη γὰρ ἔσχες ἐλπίδ᾽ ὡς ἐμοῦ θεοὺς
ὤραν τιν᾽ ἕξειν, ὥστε σωθῆναί ποτε;

ΙΣΜΗΝΗ

ἔγωγε τοῖς νῦν γ᾽, ὦ πάτερ, μαντεύμασιν.

ΟΙΔΙΠΟΥΣ

ποίοισι τούτοις; τί δὲ τεθέσπισται, τέκνον;

ISMENE

Father, I will not speak of what I suffered
in my attempts to find out where you live.
I do not wish to undergo that pain
a second time by telling you the story.
I came to talk about the fearful things
happening with your two ill-fated sons.
At first, being reasonable, they thought
about that old curse on the family,
how it has clung to your unlucky race,
and to make sure the city did not suffer
from pollution, they both wanted Creon
to be given the throne.[16] But now, urged on
by some god or their own corrupted minds,
these triply-wretched men are now engaged
in vicious war, trying to seize the throne
and win a tyrant's power. The younger one
has stripped his older brother, Polyneices,
of power and expelled him from his home.[17]
So Polyneices, according to what people say
throughout the city, has fled for refuge
to the Argos valley and is taking
a new wife there, a foreigner.[18] His friends
are now comrades in arms, and they intend
that Argos will soon seize Cadmean land
and win great honour or else sing their praise,
exalting them up to the heavens.[19] Father,
what I have said is not just idle chat!
No! These are desperate acts. At what point
the gods will pity you in your distress
I do not know.

OEDIPUS

Do you have some sudden hope
the gods will ever care enough about me
to grant me my salvation?

ISMENE

Yes, father,
that's what I think from recent oracles.

OEDIPUS

What are they? My child, what has been foretold?

ΙΣΜΗΝΗ

σὲ τοῖς ἐκεῖ ζητητὸν ἀνθρώποις ποτὲ
θανόντ᾽ ἔσεσθαι ζῶντά τ᾽ εὐσοίας χάριν.

ΟΙΔΙΠΟΥΣ

τίς δ᾽ ἂν τοιοῦδ᾽ ὑπ᾽ ἀνδρὸς εὖ πράξειεν ἄν;

ΙΣΜΗΝΗ

ἐν σοὶ τὰ κείνων φασὶ γίγνεσθαι κράτη.

ΟΙΔΙΠΟΥΣ

ὅτ᾽ οὐκέτ᾽ εἰμί, τηνικαῦτ᾽ ἄρ᾽ εἴμ᾽ ἀνήρ;

ΙΣΜΗΝΗ

νῦν γὰρ θεοί σ᾽ ὀρθοῦσι, πρόσθε δ᾽ ὤλλυσαν.

ΟΙΔΙΠΟΥΣ

γέροντα δ᾽ ὀρθοῦν φλαῦρον ὃς νέος πέσῃ.

ΙΣΜΗΝΗ

καὶ μὴν Κρέοντά γ᾽ ἴσθι σοι τούτων χάριν
ἥξοντα βαιοῦ κοὐχὶ μυρίου χρόνου.

ΟΙΔΙΠΟΥΣ

ὅπως τί δράσῃ, θύγατερ; ἑρμήνευέ μοι.

ΙΣΜΗΝΗ

ὥς σ᾽ ἄγχι γῆς στήσωσι Καδμείας, ὅπως
κρατῶσι μὲν σοῦ, γῆς δὲ μὴ ᾽μβαίνῃς ὅρων.

ΟΙΔΙΠΟΥΣ

ἡ δ᾽ ὠφέλησις τίς θύρασι κειμένου;

ΙΣΜΗΝΗ

κείνοις ὁ τύμβος δυστυχῶν ὁ σὸς βαρύς.

ΟΙΔΙΠΟΥΣ

κἄνευ θεοῦ τις τοῦτό γ᾽ ἂν γνώμῃ μάθοι.

ISMENE
The people of Thebes will soon seek you out,
alive or dead, for their own security.

OEDIPUS
Who might benefit from a man like me?

ISMENE
People say their power depends on you.

OEDIPUS
And so when I am no longer living,
at that point I truly become someone?

ISMENE
Yes. For the gods are now supporting you.
Earlier they were set on your destruction.

OEDIPUS
That is mean-spirited—to restore power
to an old man who in his youth was crushed.

ISMENE
Whatever the cause, you should think of this:
Creon will be coming here to deal with you—
and soon. It will not take him long.

OEDIPUS
What for?
Tell me why he would do that, my daughter.

ISMENE
To set you up near Theban territory,
so they can use their power to control you,
without you setting foot inside the state.

OEDIPUS
What help am I to them if I'm lying there
outside their borders?

ISMENE
They face disaster
should someone fail to pay your tomb due honours.

OEDIPUS
This I could assume without help from the gods.

ΙΣΜΗΝΗ

τούτου χάριν τοίνυν σε προσθέσθαι πέλας
χώρας θέλουσι, μηδ' ἵν' ἂν σαυτοῦ κρατοῖς.

ΟΙΔΙΠΟΥΣ

ἦ καὶ κατασκιῶσι Θηβαίᾳ κόνει;

ΙΣΜΗΝΗ

ἀλλ' οὐκ ἐᾷ τοὔμφυλον αἷμά σ', ὦ πάτερ.

ΟΙΔΙΠΟΥΣ

οὐκ ἆρ' ἐμοῦ γε μὴ κρατήσωσίν ποτε.

ΙΣΜΗΝΗ

ἔσται ποτ' ἆρα τοῦτο Καδμείοις βάρος.

ΟΙΔΙΠΟΥΣ

ποίας φανείσης, ὦ τέκνον, συναλλαγῆς;

ΙΣΜΗΝΗ

τῆς σῆς ὑπ' ὀργῆς, σοῖς ὅταν στῶσιν τάφοις.

ΟΙΔΙΠΟΥΣ

ἃ δ' ἐννέπεις, κλύουσα τοῦ λέγεις, τέκνον;

ΙΣΜΗΝΗ

ἀνδρῶν θεωρῶν Δελφικῆς ἀφ' ἑστίας.

ΟΙΔΙΠΟΥΣ

καὶ ταῦτ' ἐφ' ἡμῖν Φοῖβος εἰρηκὼς κυρεῖ;

ΙΣΜΗΝΗ

ὥς φασιν οἱ μολόντες εἰς Θήβης πέδον.

ΟΙΔΙΠΟΥΣ

παίδων τις οὖν ἤκουσε τῶν ἐμῶν τάδε;

ISMENE

That's why they want to keep you near their land,
but not where you might live by your own rules.

OEDIPUS

Will they bury me in Theban soil?

ISMENE

No.

That's not allowed, father. You are guilty
of killing one of your own blood.

OEDIPUS

In that case

they will never get their hands on me!

ISMENE

At some point that will be calamitous
for citizens of Thebes.

OEDIPUS

How will that happen,

my child? Under what conditions?

ISMENE

From your anger,

when they stand beside your tomb.

OEDIPUS

Tell me, Ismene,

where did you hear these things you're saying?

ISMENE

From sacred messengers when they returned
from the shrine at Delphi.

OEDIPUS

Has Phoebus uttered

all these things about me?

ISMENE

So those men said

when they came back to Thebes.

OEDIPUS

What about my sons—

has either of them heard this prophecy?

ΙΣΜΗΝΗ

ἄμφω γ᾽ ὁμοίως, κἀξεπίστασθον καλῶς.

ΟΙΔΙΠΟΥΣ

κᾆθ᾽ οἱ κάκιστοι τῶνδ᾽ ἀκούσαντες, πάρος
τοὐμοῦ πόθου προὔθεντο τὴν τυραννίδα;

ΙΣΜΗΝΗ

ἀλγῶ κλύουσα ταῦτ᾽ ἐγώ, φέρω δ᾽ ὅμως.

ΟΙΔΙΠΟΥΣ

ἀλλ᾽ οἱ θεοί σφιν μήτε τὴν πεπρωμένην
ἔριν κατασβέσειαν, ἐν τ᾽ ἐμοὶ τέλος
αὐτοῖν γένοιτο τῆσδε τῆς μάχης πέρι,
ἧς νῦν ἔχονται κἀπαναίρονται δόρυ·
ὡς οὔτ᾽ ἂν ὃς νῦν σκῆπτρα καὶ θρόνους ἔχει
μείνειεν οὔτ᾽ ἂν οὑξεληλυθὼς πάλιν
ἔλθοι ποτ᾽ αὖθις· οἵ γε τὸν φύσαντ᾽ ἐμὲ
οὕτως ἀτίμως πατρίδος ἐξωθούμενον
οὐκ ἔσχον οὐδ᾽ ἤμυναν, ἀλλ᾽ ἀνάστατος
αὐτοῖς ἐπέμφθην κἀξεκηρύχθην φυγάς.
εἴποις ἂν ὡς θέλοντι τοῦτ᾽ ἐμοὶ τότε
πόλις τὸ δῶρον εἰκότως κατῄνεσεν.
οὐ δῆτ᾽, ἐπεί τοι τὴν μὲν αὐτίχ᾽ ἡμέραν,
ὁπηνίκ᾽ ἔζει θυμός, ἥδιστον δέ μοι
τὸ κατθανεῖν ἦν καὶ τὸ λευσθῆναι πέτροις,
οὐδεὶς ἔρωτ᾽ ἐς τόνδ᾽ ἐφαίνετ᾽ ὠφελῶν·
χρόνῳ δ᾽, ὅτ᾽ ἤδη πᾶς ὁ μόχθος ἦν πέπων,
κἀμάνθανον τὸν θυμὸν ἐκδραμόντα μοι
μείζω κολαστὴν τῶν πρὶν ἡμαρτημένων,
τὸ τηνίκ᾽ ἤδη τοῦτο μὲν πόλις βίᾳ
ἤλαυνέ μ᾽ ἐκ γῆς χρόνιον, οἱ δ᾽ ἐπωφελεῖν,
οἱ τοῦ πατρός, τῷ πατρὶ δυνάμενοι, τὸ δρᾶν
οὐκ ἠθέλησαν, ἀλλ᾽ ἔπους σμικροῦ χάριν
φυγάς σφιν ἔξω πτωχὸς ἠλώμην ἀεί.

ISMENE

Yes, both of them. They know all about it.

OEDIPUS

So those two sons, the very worst of men,
heard of this, and instead of loving me,
preferred to seek the throne.[20]

ISMENE

To listen to this
is difficult, but it's the painful truth.

OEDIPUS

Well then, I pray the gods will not prevent
the predestined quarrel of these two sons.
I wish I could be the final arbiter
of this battle they are about to fight,
levelling spears against each other. For then
the one who holds the sceptre and the throne
would not survive, and the one in exile
would not be coming back. I am their father,
but when the Thebans drove me from my home
in great disgrace, they did not intervene.
Nor did they defend me. Those two looked on,
as I was exiled and the herald cried
the edict of my banishment. You might say
that that was what I wanted at the time
and thus the city did the proper thing
in granting me that gift. That is not true!
For on the very day when my heart burned
and my sweetest wish was death by stoning,
no one appeared to grant what I desired.
Later on, once all my anger ebbed away,
I thought my passionate heart had sought
a punishment too great for past mistakes,
but then the city, after all that time,
forced me out of Thebes and into exile.[21]
At that point those two sons could well have helped—
two children taking care of their own father.
But they refused! They did not say a thing,
not even one small word! By doing that,
those two abandoned me, let me wander
for all eternity an exiled beggar!

ἐκ ταῖνδε δ', οὔσαιν παρθένοιν, ὅσον φύσις
δίδωσιν αὐταῖν, καὶ τροφὰς ἔχω βίου
καὶ γῆς ἄδειαν καὶ γένους ἐπάρκεσιν·
τὼ δ' ἀντὶ τοῦ φύσαντος εἱλέσθην θρόνους
καὶ σκῆπτρα κραίνειν καὶ τυραννεύειν χθονός.
ἀλλ' οὔ τι μὴ λάχωσι τοῦδε συμμάχου,
οὐδέ σφιν ἀρχῆς τῆσδε Καδμείας ποτὲ
ὄνησις ἥξει· τοῦτ' ἐγῷδα, τῆσδέ τε
μαντεῖ' ἀκούων συννοῶν τε τἀξ ἐμοῦ
παλαίφαθ' ἁμοὶ Φοῖβος ἤνυσέν ποτε.
πρὸς ταῦτα καὶ Κρέοντα πεμπόντων ἐμοῦ
μαστῆρα, κεἴ τις ἄλλος ἐν πόλει σθένει.
ἐὰν γὰρ ὑμεῖς, ὦ ξένοι, θέληθ' ὁμοῦ
προστάτισι ταῖς σεμναῖσι δημούχοις θεαῖς
ἀλκὴν ποεῖσθαι, τῇδε τῇ πόλει μέγαν
σωτῆρ' ἀρεῖσθε, τοῖς δ' ἐμοῖς ἐχθροῖς πόνους.

Χορος

ἐπάξιος μέν, Οἰδίπους, κατοικτίσαι,
αὐτός τε παῖδές θ' αἵδ'· ἐπεὶ δὲ τῆσδε γῆς
σωτῆρα σαυτὸν τῷδ' ἐπεμβάλλεις λόγῳ,
παραινέσαι σοι βούλομαι τὰ σύμφορα.

Οιδιπους

ὦ φίλταθ', ὡς νῦν πᾶν τελοῦντι προξένει.

Χορος

θοῦ νῦν καθαρμὸν τῶνδε δαιμόνων, ἐφ' ἃς
τὸ πρῶτον ἵκου καὶ κατέστειψας πέδον.

Οιδιπους

τρόποισι ποίοις; ὦ ξένοι, διδάσκετε.

Χορος

πρῶτον μὲν ἱερὰς ἐξ ἀειρύτου χοὰς
κρήνης ἐνεγκοῦ, δι' ὁσίων χειρῶν θιγών.

It is from these two here, these girls, I get
my daily food, a secure resting place,
and family care, as much as nature
enables them to give. But their brothers
betrayed their father for throne and sceptre
and power to rule the land. Those sons of mine
will never win me as an ally—never!
And they will derive no benefits at all
from ruling Thebes as king. All this I know
from listening to this girl's prophecies
and thinking about those I remember
from long ago, which Phoebus Apollo
is now at last bringing to fruition.[22]
So let them dispatch Creon to find me,
or anyone else with power in Thebes.
If you, strangers, are willing to protect me,
assisted by these revered goddesses
who guard your people, then you will receive
a powerful saviour for the city
and cause my enemies distress.

CHORUS

Oedipus,
you have earned our sympathy, you and these girls,
and since, in addition to your story,
you offer yourself as this land's saviour,
I would like now, for your own benefit,
to offer some advice.

OEDIPUS

My dearest friends,
give me your help, and I will carry out
everything you say.

CHORUS

You must cleanse yourself
before these goddesses you first approached
and on whose grounds you trampled.

OEDIPUS

Tell me how—
instruct me, strangers, what I should perform.

CHORUS

First of all, once you have purified your hands,
bring sacred water from the ever-flowing spring.

ΟΙΔΙΠΟΥΣ

ὅταν δὲ τοῦτο χεῦμ᾽ ἀκήρατον λάβω;

ΧΟΡΟΣ

κρατῆρές εἰσιν, ἀνδρὸς εὔχειρος τέχνη,
ὧν κρᾶτ᾽ ἔρεψον καὶ λαβὰς ἀμφιστόμους.

ΟΙΔΙΠΟΥΣ

θαλλοῖσιν ἢ κρόκαισιν, ἢ ποίῳ τρόπῳ;

ΧΟΡΟΣ

οἰός γε νεαρᾶς νεοπόκῳ μαλλῷ λαβών.

ΟΙΔΙΠΟΥΣ

εἶεν· τὸ δ᾽ ἔνθεν ποῖ τελευτῆσαί με χρή;

ΧΟΡΟΣ

χοὰς χέασθαι στάντα πρὸς πρώτην ἕω.

ΟΙΔΙΠΟΥΣ

ἦ τοῖσδε κρωσσοῖς οἷς λέγεις χέω τάδε;

ΧΟΡΟΣ

τρισσάς γε πηγάς· τὸν τελευταῖον δ᾽ ὅλον.

ΟΙΔΙΠΟΥΣ

τοῦ τόνδε πλήσας θῶ; δίδασκε καὶ τόδε.

ΧΟΡΟΣ

ὕδατος, μελίσσης· μηδὲ προσφέρειν μέθυ.

ΟΙΔΙΠΟΥΣ

ὅταν δὲ τούτων γῆ μελάμφυλλος τύχῃ;

ΧΟΡΟΣ

τρὶς ἐννέ᾽ αὐτῇ κλῶνας ἐξ ἀμφοῖν χεροῖν
τιθεὶς ἐλαίας τάσδ᾽ ἐπεύχεσθαι λιτάς.

ΟΙΔΙΠΟΥΣ

τούτων ἀκοῦσαι βούλομαι· μέγιστα γάρ.

OEDIPUS
When I bring this pure water back, what then?

CHORUS
There are bowls, the work of skilful craftsmen—
cover the rims and handles on both sides.

OEDIPUS
Cover them with what? Wool or olive twigs?

CHORUS
Use wool freshly shorn from a female lamb.

OEDIPUS
All right. What next? How do I end the rite?

CHORUS
Pour your libations facing early dawn.

OEDIPUS
I pour them from the mixing bowls you mentioned?

CHORUS
Yes, from two bowls pour three separate streams,
but with the last one pour it all at once.

OEDIPUS
Before I set the third bowl with the others,
what do I fill it with? Tell me that.

CHORUS
With water and honey, but add no wine.

OEDIPUS
And when the dark leaf-covered earth has drunk,
what then?

CHORUS
With both hands set down olive twigs—
three sets of nine—while you recite this prayer . . .

OEDIPUS
I need to hear the prayer—that's most important.

ΧΟΡΟΣ

ὥς σφας καλοῦμεν Εὐμενίδας, ἐξ εὐμενῶν
στέρνων δέχεσθαι τὸν ἱκέτην σωτήριον,
αἰτοῦ σύ τ' αὐτὸς κεἴ τις ἄλλος ἀντὶ σοῦ,
ἄπυστα φωνῶν μηδὲ μηκύνων βοήν·
ἔπειτ' ἀφέρπειν ἄστροφος. καὶ ταῦτά σοι
δράσαντι θαρσῶν ἂν παρασταίην ἐγώ·
ἄλλως δὲ δειμαίνοιμ' ἄν, ὦ ξέν', ἀμφὶ σοι.

ΟΙΔΙΠΟΥΣ

ὦ παῖδε, κλύετον τῶνδε προσχώρων ξένων;

ΑΝΤΙΓΟΝΗ

ἠκούσαμέν τε χὤ τι δεῖ πρόστασσε δρᾶν.

ΟΙΔΙΠΟΥΣ

ἐμοὶ μὲν οὐχ ὁδωτά· λείπομαι γὰρ ἐν
τῷ μὴ δύνασθαι μήδ' ὁρᾶν, δυοῖν κακοῖν·
σφῷν δ' ἁτέρα μολοῦσα πραξάτω τάδε.
ἀρκεῖν γὰρ οἶμαι κἀντὶ μυρίων μίαν
ψυχὴν τάδ' ἐκτίνουσαν, ἢν εὔνους παρῇ.
ἀλλ' ἐν τάχει τι πράσσετον· μόνον δέ με
μὴ λείπετ'· οὐ γὰρ ἂν σθένοι τοὐμὸν δέμας
ἔρημον ἕρπειν οὐδ' ὑφηγητοῦ δίχα.

ΙΣΜΗΝΗ

ἀλλ' εἶμ' ἐγὼ τελοῦσα· τὸν τόπον δ' ἵνα
χρῆσταί μ' ἐφευρεῖν, τοῦτο βούλομαι μαθεῖν.

ΧΟΡΟΣ

τοὐκεῖθεν ἄλσους, ὦ ξένη, τοῦδ'· ἢν δέ του
σπάνιν τιν' ἴσχῃς, ἔστ' ἔποικος ὃς φράσει.

ΙΣΜΗΝΗ

χωροῖμ' ἂν ἐς τόδ'· Ἀντιγόνη, σὺ δ' ἐνθάδε
φύλασσε πατέρα τόνδε· τοῖς τεκοῦσι γὰρ
οὐδ' εἰ πονεῖ τις, δεῖ πόνου μνήμην ἔχειν.

CHORUS

Pray that, since we call them the Kindly Ones,
they will graciously receive a suppliant
and save him. You must make this prayer yourself
or have someone recite it in your place.
Speak so no one hears you. Don't pray out loud.
Then leave the place, and do not turn around.
If you do this, then I will have the strength
to stand beside you as your friend. If not,
then, stranger, I would be afraid for you.

OEDIPUS

Children, did you hear what the strangers said?
They live here.

ANTIGONE

We heard. Tell us what we must do.

OEDIPUS

It is not possible for me to do it,
since two afflictions render me unfit:
I am not strong enough, and I am blind.
One of you go in and perform this rite.
For I believe one heart can intercede
and atone in full for tens of thousands,
if that heart is pure. But you must hurry.
Do not leave me by myself—my body
cannot shuffle along all on its own,
not without somebody there to guide me.

ISMENE

I will go and carry out the ritual,
but where is the place? I need to know that.

CHORUS

It's over there, stranger, beyond the grove.
If you need anything, there's someone there.
He will direct you.

ISMENE

I'll go and do it.
Antigone, look after our father here.
If helping out our parents requires work,
we should not consider that a burden.

[Exit ISMENE]

ΧΟΡΟΣ

δεινὸν μὲν τὸ πάλαι κείμενον ἤδη κακόν, ὦ ξεῖν',
ἐπεγείρειν·
ὅμως δ' ἔραμαι πυθέσθαι

ΟΙΔΙΠΟΥΣ

τί τοῦτο;

ΧΟΡΟΣ

τᾶς δειλαίας ἀπόρου φανείσας
ἀλγηδόνος, ξυνέστας.

ΟΙΔΙΠΟΥΣ

μὴ πρὸς ξενίας ἀνοίξῃς
τᾶς σᾶς ἃ πέπονθ' ἀναιδῆ.

ΧΟΡΟΣ

τό τοι πολὺ καὶ μηδαμὰ λῆγον
χρῄζω, ξεῖν', ὀρθὸν ἄκουσμ' ἀκοῦσαι.

ΟΙΔΙΠΟΥΣ

ὤμοι.

ΧΟΡΟΣ

στέρξον, ἱκετεύω.

ΟΙΔΙΠΟΥΣ

φεῦ φεῦ.

ΧΟΡΟΣ

πείθου· κἀγὼ γὰρ ὅσον σὺ προσχρῄζεις.

ΟΙΔΙΠΟΥΣ

ἤνεγκ' οὖν κακότατ', ὦ ξένοι, ἤνεγκ' ἀέκων μέν,
θεὸς ἴστω,
τούτων δ' αὐθαίρετον οὐδέν.

ΧΟΡΟΣ

ἀλλ' ἐς τί;

ΟΙΔΙΠΟΥΣ

κακᾷ μ' εὐνᾷ πόλις οὐδὲν ἴδριν
γάμων ἐνέδησεν ἄτᾳ.

CHORUS

Stranger, to stir up ancient suffering
that for a long time has been lying dormant
is a dreadful thing, but I would like to know . . .

OEDIPUS

What it is?

CHORUS

. . . about those torment you endured—
the painful, inescapable regrets.

OEDIPUS

By all the laws of hospitality,
do not bring up the shame I have been through.

CHORUS

But the story is well known, and people
talk about it still. My friend, I'd like to hear
the truth about what really happened.

OEDIPUS

No, no.

CHORUS

Please tell me. I am begging you.

OEDIPUS

Alas! Alas!

CHORUS

You should grant me this request.
I have done everything you asked of me.

OEDIPUS

O my friends, I have suffered agonies,
the worst there are, but the things I did—
and may the gods be witness to my words!—
were unintentional. I did not choose
to do any of them of my own free will.

CHORUS

How did that happen?

OEDIPUS

Without my knowledge,
the city entangled me in ruin
with a disastrous marriage.

ΧΟΡΟΣ

ἦ ματρόθεν, ὡς ἀκούω,
δυσώνυμα λέκτρ᾽ ἐπλήσω;

ΟΙΔΙΠΟΥΣ

ὤμοι θάνατος μὲν τάδ᾽ ἀκούειν,
ὦ ξεῖν᾽· αὗται δὲ δύ᾽ ἐξ ἐμοῦ μὲν

ΧΟΡΟΣ

πῶς φῄς;

ΟΙΔΙΠΟΥΣ

παῖδε, δύο δ᾽ ἄτα

ΧΟΡΟΣ

ὦ Ζεῦ.

ΟΙΔΙΠΟΥΣ

ματρὸς κοινᾶς ἀπέβλαστον ὠδῖνος.

ΧΟΡΟΣ

σαί τ᾽ εἴσ᾽ ἄρ᾽ ἀπόγονοί τε καὶ

ΟΙΔΙΠΟΥΣ

κοιναί γε πατρὸς ἀδελφεαί.

ΧΟΡΟΣ

ἰώ.

ΟΙΔΙΠΟΥΣ

ἰὼ δῆτα μυρίων γ᾽ ἐπιστροφαὶ κακῶν.

ΧΟΡΟΣ

ἔπαθες

ΟΙΔΙΠΟΥΣ

ἔπαθον ἄλαστ᾽ ἔχειν.

ΧΟΡΟΣ

ἔρεξας

ΟΙΔΙΠΟΥΣ

οὐκ ἔρεξα.

CHORUS

Is it true
you shamed the marriage bed by sharing it
with your own mother? That's what people say.

OEDIPUS

Alas for me! Those are deadly words to hear!
Friends, those two girls of mine . . .

CHORUS

What are you saying?

OEDIPUS

Those two daughters—they are abominations!

CHORUS

O Zeus!

OEDIPUS

Born from their mother's agony—
the very mother who bore me as well!

CHORUS

So these young girls here are your daughters and . . .

OEDIPUS

Yes, and their father's sisters, too.

CHORUS

O god![23]

OEDIPUS

Alas! Countless torments return once more,
wheeling to attack me!

CHORUS

You have suffered . . .

OEDIPUS

What I have been through I cannot forget!

CHORUS

You have committed . . .

OEDIPUS

I have committed nothing!

ΧΟΡΟΣ

τί γάρ;

ΟΙΔΙΠΟΥΣ

ἐδεξάμην
δῶρον, ὃ μήποτ᾽ ἐγὼ ταλακάρδιος
ἐπωφέλησας πόλεος ἐξελέσθαι.

ΧΟΡΟΣ

δύστανε, τί γάρ; ἔθου φόνον

ΟΙΔΙΠΟΥΣ

τί τοῦτο; τί δ᾽ ἐθέλεις μαθεῖν;

ΧΟΡΟΣ

πατρός;

ΟΙΔΙΠΟΥΣ

παπαῖ. δευτέραν ἔπαισας, ἐπὶ νόσῳ νόσον,

ΧΟΡΟΣ

ἔκανες

ΟΙΔΙΠΟΥΣ

ἔκανον. ἔχει δέ μοι

ΧΟΡΟΣ

τί τοῦτο;

ΟΙΔΙΠΟΥΣ

πρὸς δίκας τι.

ΧΟΡΟΣ

τί γάρ;

ΟΙΔΙΠΟΥΣ

ἐγὼ φράσω.
καὶ γὰρ ἄν, οὓς ἐφόνευσ᾽, ἔμ᾽ ἀπώλεσαν·
νόμῳ δὲ καθαρός, ἄϊδρις εἰς τόδ᾽ ἦλθον.

CHORUS

What do you mean?

OEDIPUS

I received her as a gift.
How I wish, in my miserable state,
I had not taken her as my reward
for rescuing the city.[24]

CHORUS

You poor man!
What then? Did you murder . . .

OEDIPUS

What is it now?
What do you wish to know?

CHORUS

Did you kill your father?

OEDIPUS

O no, not that! You stab me once again,
wound piled on wound!

CHORUS

So then you did kill him.

OEDIPUS

I killed him. But in my defence there is . . .

CHORUS

What?

OEDIPUS

. . . something to justify my action.

CHORUS

What is that?

OEDIPUS

I will tell you. I killed men
who would have slaughtered me, and I did so
in ignorance. By law I'm innocent,
and yet I've come to this.[25]

ΧΟΡΟΣ

καὶ μὴν ἄναξ ὅδ᾽ ἡμὶν Αἰγέως γόνος
Θησεὺς κατ᾽ ὀμφὴν σὴν ἐφ᾽ ἀστάλη πάρα.

ΘΗΣΕΥΣ

πολλῶν ἀκούων ἔν τε τῷ πάρος χρόνῳ
τὰς αἱματηρὰς ὀμμάτων διαφθορὰς
ἔγνωκά σ᾽, ὦ παῖ Λαΐου, τανῦν θ᾽ ὁδοῖς
ἐν ταῖσδ᾽ ἀκούων μᾶλλον ἐξεπίσταμαι.
σκευή τε γάρ σε καὶ τὸ δύστηνον κάρα
δηλοῦτον ἡμῖν ὄνθ᾽ ὃς εἶ, καί σ᾽ οἰκτίσας
θέλω ᾽περέσθαι, δύσμορ᾽ Οἰδίπους, τίνα
πόλεως ἐπέστης προστροπὴν ἐμοῦ τ᾽ ἔχων,
αὐτός τε χὴ σὴ δύσμορος παραστάτις.
δίδασκε· δεινὴν γάρ τιν᾽ ἂν πρᾶξιν τύχοις
λέξας ὁποίας ἐξαφισταίμην ἐγώ,
ὃς οἶδα καὐτὸς ὡς ἐπαιδεύθην ξένος,
ὥσπερ σύ, χὠς εἷς πλεῖστ᾽ ἀνὴρ ἐπὶ ξένης
ἤθλησα κινδυνεύματ᾽ ἐν τὠμῷ κάρᾳ·
ὥστε ξένον γ᾽ ἂν οὐδέν᾽ ὄνθ᾽, ὥσπερ σὺ νῦν,
ὑπεκτραποίμην μὴ οὐ συνεκσῴζειν· ἐπεὶ
ἔξοιδ᾽ ἀνὴρ ὢν χὤτι τῆς εἰς αὔριον
οὐδὲν πλέον μοι σοῦ μέτεστιν ἡμέρας.

ΟΙΔΙΠΟΥΣ

Θησεῦ, τὸ σὸν γενναῖον ἐν σμικρῷ λόγῳ
παρῆκεν, ὥστε βραχέα μοι δεῖσθαι φράσαι.
σὺ γάρ μ᾽ ὅς εἰμι κἀφ᾽ ὅτου πατρὸς γεγὼς
καὶ γῆς ὁποίας ἦλθον, εἰρηκὼς κυρεῖς·
ὥστ᾽ ἐστί μοι τὸ λοιπὸν οὐδὲν ἄλλο πλὴν
εἰπεῖν ἃ χρῄζω, χὠ λόγος διοίχεται.

ΘΗΣΕΥΣ

τοῦτ᾽ αὐτὸ νῦν δίδασχ᾽, ὅπως ἂν ἐκμάθω.

CHORUS

Look over there!
Here comes Theseus, son of Aegeus,
our ruler, responding to your summons
and prepared to help.

[Enter THESEUS and ATTENDANTS]

THESEUS

In the past many men
have told me of the bloody mutilation
of your eyes, son of Laius, and what I heard
while on my way here makes me more certain
I truly recognize just who you are.
Your clothing and your ravaged features, too,
both confirm your identity for us.
I pity you, ill-fated Oedipus,
and I would like to know what petition
to me and to the city brings you here,
you and that unlucky girl beside you.
Let me hear it. You would have to mention
something outrageous for me to stand aside.
I know I myself was raised in exile,
just as you were, and in foreign countries
I struggled against many mortal dangers,
more so than any other man.[26] And thus
I would not turn away any stranger
in your position or refuse to help.
For I know well I am a mortal man,
and thus my share of what tomorrow brings
is no greater than your own.

OEDIPUS

Theseus,
the nobleness in those few words you spoke
is such that I require no long reply.
You mentioned who I am, who my father was,
and the land I come from. So there remains
nothing for me to say except to state
what I would like, and then my speech is done.

THESEUS

Well, then, say what it is, so that I know.

ΟΙΔΙΠΟΥΣ

δώσων ἱκάνω τοὐμὸν ἄθλιον δέμας
σοὶ δῶρον, οὐ σπουδαῖον εἰς ὄψιν· τὰ δὲ
κέρδη παρ᾽ αὐτοῦ κρείσσον᾽ ἢ μορφὴ καλή.

ΘΗΣΕΥΣ

ποῖον δὲ κέρδος ἀξιοῖς ἥκειν φέρων;

ΟΙΔΙΠΟΥΣ

χρόνῳ μάθοις ἄν, οὐχὶ τῷ παρόντι που.

ΘΗΣΕΥΣ

ποίῳ γὰρ ἡ σὴ προσφορὰ δηλώσεται;

ΟΙΔΙΠΟΥΣ

ὅταν θάνω ᾽γὼ καὶ σύ μου ταφεὺς γένῃ

ΘΗΣΕΥΣ

τὰ λοίσθι᾽ αἰτεῖ τοῦ βίου, τὰ δ᾽ ἐν μέσῳ
ἢ λῆστιν ἴσχεις ἢ δι᾽ οὐδενὸς ποεῖ.

ΟΙΔΙΠΟΥΣ

ἐνταῦθα γάρ μοι κεῖνα συγκομίζεται.

ΘΗΣΕΥΣ

ἀλλ᾽ ἐν βραχεῖ δὴ τήνδε μ᾽ ἐξαιτεῖ χάριν.

ΟΙΔΙΠΟΥΣ

ὅρα γε μήν· οὐ σμικρός, οὔχ, ἁγὼν ὅδε.

ΘΗΣΕΥΣ

πότερα τὰ τῶν σῶν ἐκγόνων κἀμοῦ λέγεις;

ΟΙΔΙΠΟΥΣ

κεῖνοι κομίζειν κεῖσ᾽ ἄναξ, χρῄζουσί με.

OEDIPUS

I have come here to offer you a gift,
this wretched body of mine. To look at,
it has little value, but the benefits
it confers surpass a pleasing shape.

THESEUS

You claim you bring us a great advantages.
What are they?

OEDIPUS

You may find out later on,
but not right now.

THESEUS

Well then, at what point
will this gift of yours reveal itself to us?

OEDIPUS

When I am dead and you have buried me.

THESEUS

You ask for your life's final ritual
but ignore what happens before you die,
or else you do not care.

OEDIPUS

It does not matter.
All those other things are part of my request.[27]

THESEUS

The favour you request from me is small.

OEDIPUS

But take care. This is no trivial matter—
the struggle over me will not be small.

THESEUS

Are you referring to your sons and me?

OEDIPUS

My lord, they will be seeking to force you
to send me back to Thebes.

ΘΗΣΕΥΣ

ἀλλ' εἰ θέλοντά γ' οὐδὲ σοὶ φεύγειν καλόν.

ΟΙΔΙΠΟΥΣ

ἀλλ' οὐδ', ὅτ' αὐτὸς ἤθελον, παρίεσαν.

ΘΗΣΕΥΣ

ὦ μῶρε, θυμὸς δ' ἐν κακοῖς οὐ ξύμφορον.

ΟΙΔΙΠΟΥΣ

ὅταν μάθῃς μου, νουθέτει, τανῦν δ' ἔα.

ΘΗΣΕΥΣ

δίδασκ'· ἄνευ γνώμης γὰρ οὔ με χρὴ λέγειν.

ΟΙΔΙΠΟΥΣ

πέπονθα, Θησεῦ, δεινὰ πρὸς κακοῖς κακά.

ΘΗΣΕΥΣ

ἦ τὴν παλαιὰν ξυμφορὰν γένους ἐρεῖς;

ΟΙΔΙΠΟΥΣ

οὐ δῆτ', ἐπεὶ πᾶς τοῦτό γ' Ἑλλήνων θροεῖ.

ΘΗΣΕΥΣ

τί γὰρ τὸ μεῖζον ἢ κατ' ἄνθρωπον νοσεῖς;

ΟΙΔΙΠΟΥΣ

οὕτως ἔχει μοι. γῆς ἐμῆς ἀπηλάθην
πρὸς τῶν ἐμαυτοῦ σπερμάτων· ἔστιν δέ μοι
πάλιν κατελθεῖν μήποθ', ὡς πατροκτόνῳ.

ΘΗΣΕΥΣ

πῶς δῆτα σ' ἂν πεμψαίαθ', ὥστ' οἰκεῖν δίχα;

ΟΙΔΙΠΟΥΣ

τὸ θεῖον αὐτοὺς ἐξαναγκάσει στόμα.

THESEUS

If that is what you wish,
then your banishment is not appropriate.

OEDIPUS

No! When I wanted to remain in Thebes
they would not agree!

THESEUS

You are foolish.
In times of trouble anger does not help.

OEDIPUS

Give me advice once you have heard my story.
Until then, spare me.

THESEUS

Then tell it to me.
I should not speak until I know the facts.

OEDIPUS

I have suffered dreadfully, Theseus,
evil after evil—horrific things!

THESEUS

Do you mean that ancient family curse
placed on your race?

OEDIPUS

No, not that at all.
That's something the whole of Greece talks about.

THESEUS

Then are you sick with more than mortal grief?
What it is?

OEDIPUS

My situation is this.
I was driven away from my own land
by my two sons, and I cannot return
because I killed my father.

THESEUS

But why then,
if you cannot live there, will they summon you?

OEDIPUS

The oracle of the god will force them to.

ΘΗΣΕΥΣ

ποῖον πάθος δείσαντας ἐκ χρηστηρίων;

ΟΙΔΙΠΟΥΣ

ὅτι σφ' ἀνάγκη τῇδε πληγῆναι χθονί.

ΘΗΣΕΥΣ

καὶ πῶς γένοιτ' ἂν τἀμὰ κἀκείνων πικρά;

ΟΙΔΙΠΟΥΣ

ὦ φίλτατ' Αἰγέως παῖ, μόνοις οὐ γίγνεται
θεοῖσι γῆρας οὐδὲ κατθανεῖν ποτε.
τὰ δ' ἄλλα συγχεῖ πάνθ' ὁ παγκρατὴς χρόνος.
φθίνει μὲν ἰσχὺς γῆς, φθίνει δὲ σώματος,
θνῄσκει δὲ πίστις, βλαστάνει δ' ἀπιστία,
καὶ πνεῦμα ταὐτὸν οὔποτ' οὔτ' ἐν ἀνδράσιν
φίλοις βέβηκεν οὔτε πρὸς πόλιν πόλει.
τοῖς μὲν γὰρ ἤδη, τοῖς δ' ἐν ὑστέρῳ χρόνῳ
τὰ τερπνὰ πικρὰ γίγνεται καὖθις φίλα.
καὶ ταῖσι Θήβαις εἰ τανῦν εὐημερεῖ
καλῶς τὰ πρὸς σέ, μυρίας ὁ μυρίος
χρόνος τεκνοῦται νύκτας ἡμέρας τ' ἰών,
ἐν αἷς τὰ νῦν ξύμφωνα δεξιώματα
δόρει διασκεδῶσιν ἐκ σμικροῦ λόγου·
ἵν' οὑμὸς εὕδων καὶ κεκρυμμένος νέκυς
ψυχρός ποτ' αὐτῶν θερμὸν αἷμα πίεται,
εἰ Ζεὺς ἔτι Ζεὺς χὠ Διὸς Φοῖβος σαφής.
ἀλλ' οὐ γὰρ αὐδᾶν ἡδὺ τἀκίνητ' ἔπη,
ἔα μ' ἐν οἷσιν ἠρξάμην, τὸ σὸν μόνον
πιστὸν φυλάσσων, κοὔποτ' Οἰδίπουν ἐρεῖς
ἀχρεῖον οἰκητῆρα δέξασθαι τόπων
τῶν ἐνθάδ', εἴπερ μὴ θεοὶ ψεύσουσί με.

ΧΟΡΟΣ

ἄναξ, πάλαι καὶ ταῦτα καὶ τοιαῦτ' ἔπη
γῇ τῇδ' ὅδ' ἁνὴρ ὡς τελῶν ἐφαίνετο.

THESEUS
What evil has the oracle declared
that makes them so afraid?

OEDIPUS
It prophesied
that in your country they will be defeated.

THESEUS
And how will they become my enemies?

OEDIPUS
Dearest son of Aegeus, only gods
are never troubled by old age and death.
All other things are finally destroyed
by all-conquering Time. The power of Earth
passes away, the body's strength withers,
loyalty perishes, distrust appears,
and between one city and another,
just as between good friends, relationships
never remain the same. Sooner or later
pleasant concord turns to bitter hatred
and then hatred, once again, to friendship.
So if today between yourself and Thebes
the sun is shining bright and all is well,
the endless passage of infinite Time
engenders innumerable days and nights,
and in that time some trivial reason
will persuade them to shatter with their spears
whatever treaties you now have between you.
And then, if Zeus is, at that time, still Zeus
and if his son Apollo speaks the truth,
my frigid, slumbering, and buried corpse
will drink hot Theban blood. I will not speak
of secrets that should remain unspoken,
so let me end my speech where I began:
if you will only do what you have pledged,
and if the gods are not deceiving me,
you will never say you sheltered Oedipus
here in your land and reaped no benefits.

CHORUS
My lord, this man has, from the very start,
made it clear to us he would accomplish
these and similar good things for our state.

ΘΗΣΕΥΣ

τίς δῆτ' ἂν ἀνδρὸς εὐμένειαν ἐκβάλοι
τοιοῦδ', ὅτῳ πρῶτον μὲν ἡ δορύξενος
κοινή παρ' ἡμῖν αἰέν ἐστιν ἑστία;
ἔπειτα δ' ἱκέτης δαιμόνων ἀφιγμένος
γῇ τῇδε κἀμοὶ δασμὸν οὐ σμικρὸν τίνει.
ἁγὼ σεβισθεὶς οὔποτ' ἐκβαλῶ χάριν
τὴν τοῦδε, χώρᾳ δ' ἔμπολιν κατοικιῶ.
εἰ δ' ἐνθάδ' ἡδὺ τῷ ξένῳ μίμνειν, σέ νιν
τάξω φυλάσσειν, εἴτ' ἐμοῦ στείχειν μέτα,
τόδ' ἡδύ, τούτων, Οἰδίπους, δίδωμί σοι
κρίναντι χρῆσθαι· τῇδε γὰρ ξυνοίσομαι.

ΟΙΔΙΠΟΥΣ

ὦ Ζεῦ, διδοίης τοῖσι τοιούτοισιν εὖ.

ΘΗΣΕΥΣ

τί δῆτα χρῄζεις; ἦ δόμους στείχειν ἐμούς;

ΟΙΔΙΠΟΥΣ

εἴ μοι θέμις γ' ἦν· ἀλλ' ὁ χῶρός ἐσθ' ὅδε,

ΘΗΣΕΥΣ

ἐν ᾧ τί πράξεις; οὐ γὰρ ἀντιστήσομαι.

ΟΙΔΙΠΟΥΣ

ἐν ᾧ κρατήσω τῶν ἔμ' ἐκβεβληκότων.

ΘΗΣΕΥΣ

μέγ' ἂν λέγοις δώρημα τῆς συνουσίας.

ΟΙΔΙΠΟΥΣ

εἰ σοί γ' ἅπερ φῂς ἐμμενεῖ τελοῦντί μοι.

ΘΗΣΕΥΣ

θάρσει τὸ τοῦδέ γ' ἀνδρός· οὔ σε μὴ προδῶ.

ΟΙΔΙΠΟΥΣ

οὔτοι σ' ὑφ' ὅρκου γ' ὡς κακὸν πιστώσομαι.

THESEUS

Who then would repudiate the friendship
of a man like this, one for whom, first of all,
an ally's hearth, by mutual agreement,
is always welcoming? Then he has come
as a suppliant to our gods and offers
no small reward to this land and to me.
I respect these things—I will never spurn
the favours of this man. I will establish
a place here he may live as a citizen.
If the stranger wishes to remain here,
I will appoint you his protectors. But if
he would prefer to, he can come with me.
Choose the option you think best, Oedipus.
Whatever choice you make will be my own.

OEDIPUS

O Zeus, be gracious to such men as these!

THESEUS

What would you like? To come back to my home?

OEDIPUS

I would, if that had been ordained for me.
But this is the place . . .

THESEUS

What will you do here?
Speak up. I will not countermand your choice.

OEDIPUS

. . . where I will conquer those who drove me out.

THESEUS

If so, your presence here would prove to be
a major benefit for us.

OEDIPUS

It will,
if you fulfil your promises to me.

THESEUS

Have faith in me. I will not let you down.

OEDIPUS

I will not ask you to confirm your pledge
with an oath, as one does with wicked men.

ΘΗΣΕΥΣ

οὔκουν πέρα γ᾽ ἂν οὐδὲν ἢ λόγῳ φέροις.

ΟΙΔΙΠΟΥΣ

πῶς οὖν ποήσεις;

ΘΗΣΕΥΣ

τοῦ μάλιστ᾽ ὄκνος σ᾽ ἔχει;

ΟΙΔΙΠΟΥΣ

ἥξουσιν ἄνδρες

ΘΗΣΕΥΣ

ἀλλὰ τοῖσδ᾽ ἔσται μέλον.

ΟΙΔΙΠΟΥΣ

ὅρα με λείπων

ΘΗΣΕΥΣ

μὴ δίδασχ᾽ ἃ χρή με δρᾶν.

ΟΙΔΙΠΟΥΣ

ὀκνοῦντ᾽ ἀνάγκη.

ΘΗΣΕΥΣ

τοὐμὸν οὐκ ὀκνεῖ κέαρ.

ΟΙΔΙΠΟΥΣ

οὐκ οἶσθ᾽ ἀπειλὰς

ΘΗΣΕΥΣ

οἶδ᾽ ἐγώ σε μή τινα
ἐνθένδ᾽ ἀπάξοντ᾽ ἄνδρα πρὸς βίαν ἐμοῦ.
πολλαὶ δ᾽ ἀπειλαὶ πολλὰ δὴ μάτην ἔπη
θυμῷ κατηπείλησαν, ἀλλ᾽ ὁ νοῦς ὅταν
αὑτοῦ γένηται, φροῦδα τἀπειλήματα.
κείνοις δ᾽ ἴσως κεἰ δείν᾽ ἐπερρώσθη λέγειν
τῆς σῆς ἀγωγῆς, οἶδ᾽ ἐγώ, φανήσεται
μακρὸν τὸ δεῦρο πέλαγος οὐδὲ πλώσιμον.
θαρσεῖν μὲν οὖν ἔγωγε κἂν ἐμῆς ἄνευ
γνώμης ἐπαινῶ, Φοῖβος εἰ προὔπεμψέ σε·

THESEUS
An oath would be no more reliable
than giving you my word.

OEDIPUS
What will you do?

THESEUS
What precisely do you fear?

OEDIPUS
Men will come . . .

THESEUS
But these people here will deal with them.

OEDIPUS
Be careful when you leave me.

THESEUS
There is no need
to instruct me in what I have to do.

OEDIPUS
My fear drives me to do it.

THESEUS
But my heart
has no fear.

OEDIPUS
You know nothing of their threats.

THESEUS
But I do know this: no one will carry you
away from here without permission from me.
Often men utter threats from angry hearts
in loud and empty words, but when their minds
regain control once more, their threats are gone.
And if those men are bold enough to act
on threats they made to take you back by force,
they will, I tell you, sail into rough seas
on their harsh journey here. You must take heart.
That's my advice—even without my pledge—
if Phoebus was the one who led you here.

ὅμως δὲ κἀμοῦ μὴ παρόντος οἶδ᾽ ὅτι
τοὐμὸν φυλάξει σ᾽ ὄνομα μὴ πάσχειν κακῶς.

Χοροσ

εὐίππου, ξένε, τᾶσδε χώρας
ἵκου τὰ κράτιστα γᾶς ἔπαυλα,
τὸν ἀργῆτα Κολωνόν, ἔνθ᾽
ἁ λίγεια μινύρεται
θαμίζουσα μάλιστ᾽ ἀηδὼν
χλωραῖς ὑπὸ βάσσαις,
τὸν οἰνωπὸν ἔχουσα κισσὸν
καὶ τὰν ἄβατον θεοῦ
φυλλάδα μυριόκαρπον ἀνήλιον
ἀνήνεμόν τε πάντων
χειμώνων· ἵν᾽ ὁ βακχιώτας
ἀεὶ Διόνυσος ἐμβατεύει
θεαῖς ἀμφιπολῶν τιθήναις.

θάλλει δ᾽ οὐρανίας ὑπ᾽ ἄχνας
ὁ καλλίβοτρυς κατ᾽ ἦμαρ ἀεὶ
νάρκισσος, μεγάλαιν θεαῖν
ἀρχαῖον στεφάνωμ᾽, ὅ τε
χρυσαυγὴς κρόκος· οὐδ᾽ ἄϋπνοι
κρῆναι μινύθουσιν
Κηφισοῦ νομάδες ῥεέθρων,
ἀλλ᾽ αἰὲν ἐπ᾽ ἤματι
ὠκυτόκος πεδίων ἐπινίσσεται
ἀκηράτῳ σὺν ὄμβρῳ
στερνούχου χθονός· οὐδὲ Μουσᾶν
χοροί νιν ἀπεστύγησαν οὐδ᾽ ἁ
χρυσάνιος Ἀφροδίτα.

ἔστιν δ᾽ οἷον ἐγὼ γᾶς Ἀσίας οὐκ ἐπακούω
οὐδ᾽ ἐν τᾷ μεγάλᾳ Δωρίδι νάσῳ Πέλοπος πώποτε βλαστὸν
φύτευμ᾽ ἀχείρωτον αὐτόποιον,
ἐγχέων φόβημα δαΐων,
ὃ τᾷδε θάλλει μέγιστα χώρᾳ,
γλαυκᾶς παιδοτρόφου φύλλον ἐλαίας·

And though I am elsewhere, I know my name
will nonetheless protect you from all harm.

[Exit THESEUS]

CHORUS

Stranger, in this land famed for horses
you have reached bright Colonus,
earth's finest home. Here the nightingale,
always chants her sweet, sharp melodies,
from deep within green forest groves,
living among the wine-dark ivy vines,
fruit-rich foliage of the god, a place
where no sun penetrates, no winds blow
in any storm, and no man ever treads.
Here Dionysus, the Bacchic reveller,
always roams with his companions,
the nymphs who nursed him as a child.[28]

And every day narcissus flowers bloom
in lovely clusters fed on heavenly dew,
the ancient crown of two great goddesses,
as does the glistening gold crocus, too.[29]
The sleepless fountains never fail to feed
the wandering waters of the Cephisus,
whose pure, clear stream flows every day
across the ample bosom of the land,
bringing rich nourishment to the plain.
Nor do the Muses' dancing choruses
or Aphrodite of the golden reins
fail to grant their favours to this land.

And here we have a certain kind of plant—
I have not heard of it in Asian lands,
nor does it thrive in that great Dorian isle
of Pelops. It grows without man's help,
renews itself, and terrifies our foes.
This plant truly flourishes in our land,
the gray-leafed olive tree, nurturing
our country's youth.[30] No young person here

τὸ μέν τις οὐ νεαρὸς οὐδὲ γήρᾳ
συνναίων ἁλιώσει χερὶ πέρσας· ὁ γὰρ αἰὲν ὁρῶν κύκλος
λεύσσει νιν μορίου Διὸς
χἁ γλαυκῶπις Ἀθάνα.

ἄλλον δ' αἶνον ἔχω ματροπόλει τᾷδε κράτιστον
δῶρον τοῦ μεγάλου δαίμονος, εἰπεῖν, χθονὸς αὔχημα
  μέγιστον,
εὔιππον, εὔπωλον, εὐθάλασσον.
ὦ παῖ Κρόνου, σὺ γάρ νιν εἰς
τόδ' εἷσας αὔχημ', ἄναξ Ποσειδάν,
ἵπποισιν τὸν ἀκεστῆρα χαλινὸν
πρώταισι ταῖσδε κτίσας ἀγυιαῖς.
ἁ δ' εὐήρετμος ἔκπαγλ' ἁλία χερσὶ παραπτομένα πλάτα
θρῴσκει, τῶν ἑκατομπόδων
Νηρῄδων ἀκόλουθος.

ΑΝΤΙΓΟΝΗ

ὦ πλεῖστ' ἐπαίνοις εὐλογούμενον πέδον,
νῦν σὸν τὰ λαμπρὰ ταῦτα δὴ φαίνειν ἔπη.

ΟΙΔΙΠΟΥΣ

τί δ' ἔστιν, ὦ παῖ, καινόν;

ΑΝΤΙΓΟΝΗ

ἆσσον ἔρχεται
Κρέων ὅδ' ἡμῖν οὐκ ἄνευ πομπῶν, πάτερ.

ΟΙΔΙΠΟΥΣ

ὦ φίλτατοι γέροντες, ἐξ ὑμῶν ἐμοὶ
φαίνοιτ' ἂν ἤδη τέρμα τῆς σωτηρίας.

ΧΟΡΟΣ

θάρσει, παρέσται· καὶ γὰρ εἰ γέρων ἐγώ,
τὸ τῆσδε χώρας οὐ γεγήρακεν σθένος.

ΚΡΕΩΝ

ἄνδρες χθονὸς τῆσδ' εὐγενεῖς οἰκήτορες,
ὁρῶ τιν' ὑμᾶς ὀμμάτων εἰληφότας
φόβον νεώρη τῆς ἐμῆς ἐπεισόδου,

will lift a hand to damage or destroy it,
nor any citizen living with old age,
for it guarded by the ever-watchful gaze
of grey-eyed Athena and protector Zeus.[31]

I have more praises for our mother state,
a tribute to those most glorious gifts
from a mighty god, our country's proudest boast—
the great strength of our colts and stallions
and the great power of the sea. For you,
my lord Poseidon, Cronos' son, placed her
on that proud throne and first introduced
into our roads the bridle and the bit
that curb the wildness in our horses.
You trained our hands to ply the flashing oar
and race in wonder over open seas,
chasing sea nymphs dancing in the waves,
the fifty daughters of Nereus.[32]

ANTIGONE

O Athens, land praised more than any other,
now is the time to show in how you act
just what such splendid commendations mean.

OEDIPUS

What's happening, my child?

ANTIGONE

It's Creon, father.
He's coming towards us—and with an escort.

OEDIPUS

O you old men, my dearest friends, may you now
make good that final pledge of yours and save me!

CHORUS

Take heart—our pledge still stands. We may have aged,
but still our country's strength has not grown old.

[Enter CREON with an escort]

CREON

You men, noble inhabitants of this land,
from your eyes I see that my arrival
has gripped you all with unexpected fear.

ὃν μήτ᾽ ὀκνεῖτε μήτ᾽ ἀφῆτ᾽ ἔπος κακόν.
ἥκω γὰρ οὐχ ὡς δρᾶν τι βουληθείς, ἐπεὶ
γέρων μέν εἰμι, πρὸς πόλιν δ᾽ ἐπίσταμαι
σθένουσαν ἥκων, εἴ τιν᾽ Ἑλλάδος, μέγα.
ἀλλ᾽ ἄνδρα τόνδε τηλικόσδ᾽ ἀπεστάλην
πείσων ἕπεσθαι πρὸς τὸ Καδμείων πέδον,
οὐκ ἐξ ἑνὸς στείλαντος, ἀλλ᾽ ἀνδρῶν ὑπὸ
πάντων κελευσθείς, οὕνεχ᾽ ἧκέ μοι γένει
τὰ τοῦδε πενθεῖν πήματ᾽ εἰς πλεῖστον πόλεως.
ἀλλ᾽ ὦ ταλαίπωρ᾽ Οἰδίπους, κλύων ἐμοῦ
ἱκοῦ πρὸς οἴκους. πᾶς σε Καδμείων λεὼς
καλεῖ δικαίως, ἐκ δὲ τῶν μάλιστ᾽ ἐγώ,
ὅσῳπερ, εἰ μὴ πλεῖστον ἀνθρώπων ἔφυν
κάκιστος, ἀλγῶ τοῖσι σοῖς κακοῖς, γέρον,
ὁρῶν σε τὸν δύστηνον ὄντα μὲν ξένον,
ἀεὶ δ᾽ ἀλήτην κἀπὶ προσπόλου μιᾶς
βιοστερῆ χωροῦντα· τὴν ἐγὼ τάλας
οὐκ ἄν ποτ᾽ ἐς τοσοῦτον αἰκίας πεσεῖν
ἔδοξ᾽, ὅσον πέπτωκεν ἥδε δύσμορος,
ἀεί σε κηδεύουσα καὶ τὸ σὸν κάρα
πτωχῷ διαίτῃ, τηλικοῦτος, οὐ γάμων
ἔμπειρος, ἀλλὰ τοὐπιόντος ἁρπάσαι.
ἆρ᾽ ἄθλιον τοὔνειδος, ὦ τάλας ἐγώ,
ὠνείδισ᾽ εἰς σὲ κἀμὲ καὶ τὸ πᾶν γένος;
ἀλλ᾽ οὐ γὰρ ἔστι τἀμφανῆ κρύπτειν, σύ νιν
πρὸς θεῶν πατρῴων, Οἰδίπους, πεισθεὶς ἐμοὶ
κρύψον, θελήσας ἄστυ καὶ δόμους μολεῖν
τοὺς σοὺς πατρῴους, τήνδε τὴν πόλιν φίλως
εἰπών· ἐπαξία γάρ· ἡ δ᾽ οἴκοι πλέον
δίκῃ σέβοιτ᾽ ἄν, οὖσα σὴ πάλαι τροφός.

ΟΙΔΙΠΟΥΣ

ὦ πάντα τολμῶν κἀπὸ παντὸς ἂν φέρων
λόγου δικαίου μηχάνημα ποικίλον,

Do not shrink back or utter hostile words,
for I do not come intending to use force.
I am an old man, and I understand
that if any state in Greece is truly strong
it is the powerful city I have reached.
No. I have been sent here, old though I am,
to convince this man to return to Thebes.
I was not dispatched by just one person,
but by the wish of all the citizens,
and more than any other man in Thebes
it falls on me to grieve for his misfortune,
because he is a relative of mine.[33]
O you, poor miserable Oedipus,
hear what I have to say and come back home!
Cadmeans are all summoning you back—
and justly so—I more than all the rest.[34]
I would be the very worst of all men born
if I did not find your suffering painful,
seeing you, old man, a wretched outcast,
an eternal wanderer and beggar,
stumbling around with one young girl for help.
Alas, I never thought that she would fall
into such degrading misery as this—
the poor creature, living like a vagrant,
always nursing you in your condition.
She's of marriageable age, but unwed,
there for some passing man to violate.
In pointing out all these misfortunes,
am I not casting a disgraceful slur
on you and me and our whole family line?
But no one can conceal a public shame.
So, Oedipus, by our ancestral gods,
listen to what I say—hide our disgrace
by agreeing to return to Thebes, the home
of your own ancestors. Bid this place here
a fond farewell—these men have earned your thanks.
But your own homeland merits more respect,
because she nursed you all those years ago.

OEDIPUS

You are crass enough to try anything,
even to base your devious intent

τί ταῦτα πειρᾷ κἀμὲ δεύτερον θέλεις
ἑλεῖν ἐν οἷς μάλιστ' ἂν ἀλγοίην ἁλούς;
πρόσθεν τε γάρ με τοῖσιν οἰκείοις κακοῖς
νοσοῦνθ', ὅτ' ἦν μοι τέρψις ἐκπεσεῖν χθονός,
οὐκ ἤθελες θέλοντι προσθέσθαι χάριν·
ἀλλ' ἡνίκ' ἤδη μεστὸς ἦ θυμούμενος
καὶ τοὺν δόμοισιν ἦν διαιτᾶσθαι γλυκύ,
τότ' ἐξεώθεις κἀξέβαλλες, οὐδέ σοι
τὸ συγγενὲς τοῦτ' οὐδαμῶς τότ' ἦν φίλον·
νῦν τ' αὖθις ἡνίκ' εἰσορᾷς πόλιν τέ μοι
ξυνοῦσαν εὔνουν τήνδε καὶ γένος τὸ πᾶν,
πειρᾷ μετασπᾶν, σκληρὰ μαλθακῶς λέγων.
καίτοι τίς αὕτη τέρψις ἄκοντας φιλεῖν;
ὥσπερ τις εἴ σοι λιπαροῦντι μὲν τυχεῖν
μηδὲν διδοίη μηδ' ἐπαρκέσαι θέλοι,
πλήρη δ' ἔχοντι θυμὸν ὧν χρῄζοις, τότε
δωροῖθ', ὅτ' οὐδὲν ἡ χάρις χάριν φέροι·
ἆρ' ἂν ματαίου τῆσδ' ἂν ἡδονῆς τύχοις;
τοιαῦτα μέντοι καὶ σὺ προσφέρεις ἐμοί,
λόγῳ μὲν ἐσθλά. τοῖσι δ' ἔργοισιν κακά.
φράσω δὲ καὶ τοῖσδ', ὥς σε δηλώσω κακόν.
ἥκεις ἔμ' ἄξων, οὐχ ἵν' ἐς δόμους ἄγῃς,
ἀλλ' ὡς πάραυλον οἰκίσῃς, πόλις δέ σοι
κακῶν ἄνατος τῆσδ' ἀπαλλαχθῇ χθονός.
οὐκ ἔστι σοι ταῦτ', ἀλλά σοι τάδ' ἔστ', ἐκεῖ
χώρας ἀλάστωρ οὑμὸς ἐνναίων ἀεί·
ἔστιν δὲ παισὶ τοῖς ἐμοῖσι τῆς ἐμῆς
χθονὸς λαχεῖν τοσοῦτον, ἐνθανεῖν μόνον.
ἆρ' οὐκ ἄμεινον ἢ σὺ τἀν Θήβαις φρονῶ;

on pleas for justice! Why are you doing this?
Why do you wish to catch me once again
in a snare that will bring me still more grief?
Back when I was suffering from the pain
I brought upon myself, I yearned to leave,
to be driven from Thebes, but you refused!
That favour you were not prepared to grant.
Later, once my anger had run its course
and I desired to live in my own home,
you cast me out, forced me into exile.
At that time you were not concerned at all
with those common kinship ties you mention.
Now here we are again. When you can see
how this city and its inhabitants
are all offering me their hospitality,
you try to snatch me back once more, voicing
your vicious wish in a sweet-sounding speech.
And yet what pleasure do you get from this,
welcoming me as a guest against my will?
It's as if you kept pleading with someone
to grant a favour but he was unwilling
and refused to help, and then later on,
once your spirit had everything you wished,
he granted your request, when such kindness
would not be kind at all. In such a case,
would not your joy be empty? Nonetheless,
that is what you are offering me now—
noble-sounding speeches and deceitful acts.
I will explain that to these people here
to show what a dishonest man you are.
You have not come to lead me to my home,
but to take me into custody, to set me
near your borders, so the city of Thebes
may escape unharmed any future troubles
coming from this land. But you will not succeed.
Instead of that what you will get is this:
my vengeful ghost haunting your land forever
and for my sons this legacy from me,
as much of my own land as they will need
to lie on when they die, no more than that.
As far as Thebes' future is concerned,
Creon, am I not a wiser man than you?

πολλῷ γ', ὅσῳπερ κἀκ σαφεστέρων κλύω,
Φοίβου τε καὐτοῦ Ζηνός, ὃς κείνου πατήρ.
τὸ σὸν δ' ἀφῖκται δεῦρ' ὑπόβλητον στόμα,
πολλὴν ἔχον στόμωσιν· ἐν δὲ τῷ λέγειν
κάκ' ἂν λάβοις τὰ πλείον' ἢ σωτήρια.
ἡμᾶς δ' ἔα ζῆν ἐνθάδ'· οὐ γὰρ ἂν κακῶς
οὐδ' ὧδ' ἔχοντες ζῷμεν, εἰ τερποίμεθα.

ΚΡΕΩΝ

πότερα νομίζεις δυστυχεῖν ἔμ' ἐς τὰ σά,
ἢ σ' εἰς τὰ σαυτοῦ μᾶλλον, ἐς τῷ νῦν λόγῳ;

ΟΙΔΙΠΟΥΣ

ἐμοὶ μέν ἐσθ' ἥδιστον, εἰ σὺ μήτ' ἐμὲ
πείθειν οἷός τ' εἶ μήτε τούσδε τοὺς πέλας.

ΚΡΕΩΝ

ὦ δύσμορ', οὐδὲ τῷ χρόνῳ φύσας φανεῖ
φρένας ποτ' ἀλλὰ λῦμα τῷ γήρᾳ τρέφει;

ΟΙΔΙΠΟΥΣ

γλώσσῃ σὺ δεινός· ἄνδρα δ' οὐδέν' οἶδ' ἐγὼ
δίκαιον ὅστις ἐξ ἅπαντος εὖ λέγει.

ΚΡΕΩΝ

χωρὶς τό τ' εἰπεῖν πολλὰ καὶ τὰ καίρια.

ΟΙΔΙΠΟΥΣ

ὡς δὴ σὺ βραχέα, ταῦτα δ' ἐν καιρῷ λέγεις.

ΚΡΕΩΝ

οὐ δῆθ' ὅτῳ γε νοῦς ἴσος καὶ σοὶ πάρα.

ΟΙΔΙΠΟΥΣ

ἄπελθ', ἐρῶ γὰρ καὶ πρὸ τῶνδε, μηδέ με
φύλασσ' ἐφορμῶν ἔνθα χρὴ ναίειν ἐμέ.

Yes, much wiser—since those I listen to
are the most knowledgeable ones of all,
Phoebus Apollo and his father Zeus.
You come here with that corrupt tongue of yours
honed sharp as hardened steel, but what you say
will bring you grief rather than salvation.
I know these words of mine will not convince you,
so you should leave. Let us keep living here.
To exist like this would not be difficult,
not if it brought enjoyment and content.

Creon

In this debate, which one of us do you think
has more to lose by what you are doing,
you or me?

Oedipus

For me the sweetest outcome
will be when you fail to win me over
or to convince the people standing here.

Creon

You poor man! Will you make a public show
of how in all these years you have learned nothing?
Will you keep on disgracing your old age?

Oedipus

You have a glib tongue, but I do not know
any righteous man who can argue well
and in support of every point of view.

Creon

One can say a lot and yet avoid the issue.

Oedipus

As if your speech was short and to the point!

Creon

That is not possible with minds like yours.

Oedipus

Go away! I speak for these men here, as well.
And do not try to set up a blockade
and spy on me where I am meant to live.

ΚΡΕΩΝ

μαρτύρομαι τούσδ᾽, οὐ σέ· πρὸς δὲ τοὺς φίλους
οἷ᾽ ἀνταμείβει ῥήματ᾽, ἤν σ᾽ ἕλω ποτέ—

ΟΙΔΙΠΟΥΣ

τίς δ᾽ ἄν με τῶνδε συμμάχων ἕλοι βίᾳ;

ΚΡΕΩΝ

ἦ μὴν σὺ κἄνευ τοῦδε λυπηθεὶς ἔσει.

ΟΙΔΙΠΟΥΣ

ποίῳ σὺν ἔργῳ τοῦτ᾽ ἀπειλήσας ἔχεις;

ΚΡΕΩΝ

παίδοιν δυοῖν σοι τὴν μὲν ἀρτίως ἐγὼ
ξυναρπάσας ἔπεμψα, τὴν δ᾽ ἄξω τάχα.

ΟΙΔΙΠΟΥΣ

οἴμοι.

ΚΡΕΩΝ

τάχ᾽ ἕξεις μᾶλλον οἰμώζειν τάδε.

ΟΙΔΙΠΟΥΣ

τὴν παῖδ᾽ ἔχεις μου;

ΚΡΕΩΝ

τήνδε τ᾽ οὐ μακροῦ χρόνου.

ΟΙΔΙΠΟΥΣ

ἰὼ ξένοι, τί δράσετ᾽; ἦ προδώσετε,
κοὐκ ἐξελᾶτε τὸν ἀσεβῆ τῆσδε χθονός;

ΧΟΡΟΣ

χώρει, ξέν᾽, ἔξω θᾶσσον. οὔτε γὰρ τὰ νῦν
δίκαια πράσσεις οὔθ᾽ ἃ πρόσθεν εἴργασαι.

ΚΡΕΩΝ

ὑμῖν ἂν εἴη τήνδε καιρὸς ἐξάγειν
ἄκουσαν, εἰ θέλουσα μὴ πορεύεται.

CREON
I call on these men—not on you—to witness
the way you answer your own family friends.
If I ever capture you . . . [35]

OEDIPUS
Who could seize me
if these men, my allies, are unwilling?

CREON
Even without that you will still suffer!

OEDIPUS
You are threatening me? What will you do?

CREON
I have just seized one of your two daughters
and sent her away. Soon I'll take the other.

OEDIPUS
No!

CREON
Before long you'll have more to cry about.

OEDIPUS
You have taken my daughter?

CREON
Yes I have.
And soon enough I'll have this other one.

OEDIPUS
Alas, strangers, what are you going to do?
Will you abandon me? Will you not drive
this sacrilegious man away from here?

CHORUS *[to Creon]*
You must leave here, stranger—without delay!
What you have just done and are doing now
is not acceptable.

CREON *[to his escort]*
If this young girl
does not wish to come with us, it's now time
for you to take her into custody
against her will.

ΑΝΤΙΓΟΝΗ

οἴμοι τάλαινα, ποῖ φύγω; ποίαν λάβω
θεῶν ἄρηξιν ἢ βροτῶν;

ΧΟΡΟΣ

τί δρᾷς, ξένε;

ΚΡΕΩΝ

οὐχ ἅψομαι τοῦδ᾽ ἀνδρός, ἀλλὰ τῆς ἐμῆς.

ΟΙΔΙΠΟΥΣ

ὦ γῆς ἄνακτες.

ΧΟΡΟΣ

ὦ ξέν᾽, οὐ δίκαια δρᾷς.

ΚΡΕΩΝ

δίκαια.

ΧΟΡΟΣ

πῶς δίκαια;

ΚΡΕΩΝ

τοὺς ἐμοὺς ἄγω.

ΟΙΔΙΠΟΥΣ

ἰὼ πόλις.

ΧΟΡΟΣ

τί δρᾷς, ὦ ξέν᾽; οὐκ ἀφήσεις; τάχ᾽ εἰς βάσανον εἶ
χερῶν.

ΚΡΕΩΝ

εἴργου.

ΧΟΡΟΣ

σοῦ μὲν οὔ, τάδε γε μωμένου.

ΚΡΕΩΝ

πόλει μαχεῖ γάρ, εἴ τι πημανεῖς ἐμέ.

ANTIGONE

This is insufferable!
Where can I run to? Who will help me now,
what gods or men?

CHORUS *[to Creon]*

Stranger, what are you doing?

CREON *[to the Chorus Leader]*

I will not lay a finger on this man here,
but I will take her. She belongs to me.

[CREON and his ESCORT move to apprehend ANTIGONE]

OEDIPUS

O you who rule this land!

CHORUS

These acts of yours,
stranger, are not just.

CREON

They are quite legal.

CHORUS

How are they legal?

CREON

I am taking what is mine.

OEDIPUS

Help us, Athens!

CHORUS

Stranger, what are you doing?
Leave her alone—or else you'll quickly face
a test where we resolve this in a fight.

CREON

Stay back!

CHORUS

Not if you keep acting in this way.

CREON

If you harm me, you'll be at war with Thebes.

ΟΙΔΙΠΟΥΣ

οὐκ ἠγόρευον ταῦτ᾽ ἐγώ;

ΧΟΡΟΣ

μέθες χεροῖν

τὴν παῖδα θᾶσσον.

ΚΡΕΩΝ

μὴ 'πίτασσ᾽ ἃ μὴ κρατεῖς.

ΧΟΡΟΣ

χαλᾶν λέγω σοι.

ΚΡΕΩΝ

σοὶ δ᾽ ἔγωγ᾽ ὁδοιπορεῖν.

ΧΟΡΟΣ

πρόβαθ᾽ ὧδε, βᾶτε βᾶτ᾽, ἔντοποι·
πόλις ἐναίρεται, πόλις ἐμά, σθένει· πρόβαθ᾽ ὧδέ μοι.

ΑΝΤΙΓΟΝΗ

ἀφέλκομαι δύστηνος, ὦ ξένοι ξένοι.

ΟΙΔΙΠΟΥΣ

ποῦ, τέκνον, εἶ μοι;

ΑΝΤΙΓΟΝΗ

πρὸς βίαν πορεύομαι.

ΟΙΔΙΠΟΥΣ

ὄρεξον, ὦ παῖ, χεῖρας.

ΑΝΤΙΓΟΝΗ

ἀλλ᾽ οὐδὲν σθένω.

ΚΡΕΩΝ

οὐκ ἄξεθ᾽ ὑμεῖς;

ΟΙΔΙΠΟΥΣ

ὦ τάλας ἐγώ, τάλας.

OEDIPUS
Is that not just what I predicted?

[Members of CREON'S ESCORT seize ANTIGONE]

CHORUS
Let go!
Take your hands off that girl immediately!

CREON
Do not give orders to those you do not rule.

CHORUS
I'm telling you to let that young girl go.

CREON *[to one of his soldiers holding Antigone]*
And I am ordering you to take her off.

[The ESCORT starts to drag ANTIGONE away]

CHORUS
Come here, you citizens of Colonus!
Come here and help! The city—our city—
is being violently attacked! Help us!

ANTIGONE
It's over for me—I'm being dragged away!
O you strangers, you are our hosts and friends . . .

OEDIPUS
Where are you, my child?

ANTIGONE
They're forcing me to go.

OEDIPUS
Give me your hand!

ANTIGONE
I can't—I haven't got the strength.

CREON
You men, take her away!

OEDIPUS
Alas, I'm finished!

ΚΡΕΩΝ

οὔκουν ποτ᾽ ἐκ τούτοιν γε μὴ σκήπτροιν ἔτι
ὁδοιπορήσῃς· ἀλλ᾽ ἐπεὶ νικᾶν θέλεις
πατρίδα τε τὴν σὴν καὶ φίλους, ὑφ᾽ ὧν ἐγὼ
ταχθεὶς τάδ᾽ ἔρδω, καὶ τύραννος ὢν ὅμως,
νίκα. χρόνῳ γάρ, οἶδ᾽ ἐγώ, γνώσει τάδε,
ὁθούνεκ᾽ αὐτὸς αὑτὸν οὔτε νῦν καλὰ
δρᾷς οὔτε πρόσθεν εἰργάσω βίᾳ φίλων,
ὀργῇ χάριν δούς, ἥ σ᾽ ἀεὶ λυμαίνεται.

ΧΟΡΟΣ

ἐπίσχες αὐτοῦ, ξεῖνε.

ΚΡΕΩΝ

μὴ ψαύειν λέγω.

ΧΟΡΟΣ

οὔτοι σ᾽ ἀφήσω, τῶνδέ γ᾽ ἐστερημένος.

ΚΡΕΩΝ

καὶ μεῖζον ἆρα ῥύσιον πόλει τάχα
θήσεις· ἐφάψομαι γὰρ οὐ ταύταιν μόναιν.

ΧΟΡΟΣ

ἀλλ᾽ ἐς τί τρέψει;

ΚΡΕΩΝ

τόνδ᾽ ἀπάξομαι λαβών.

ΧΟΡΟΣ

δεινὸν λέγοις ἄν.

ΚΡΕΩΝ

τοῦτο νῦν πεπράξεται.

ΧΟΡΟΣ

ἢν μή σ᾽ ὁ κραίνων τῆσδε γῆς ἀπειργάθῃ.

ΟΙΔΙΠΟΥΣ

ὦ φθέγμ᾽ ἀναιδές, ἦ σὺ γὰρ ψαύσεις ἐμοῦ;

[Creon's SOLDIERS take ANTIGONE away]

CREON

You will not be stumbling around again
using these two young girls as your support.
But since you wish to win a victory
over your native country and your friends,
on whose behalf I undertook these acts,
though I am their king, enjoy your triumph.
I know in time to come you'll recognize
how in all your actions, now and in the past,
you have not acted well by giving in,
despite your friends, to your own temper.
That has always led you to disaster.[36]

[The CHORUS moves to block CREON from leaving.]

CHORUS

Stop there, stranger!

CREON

I warn you: do not touch me!

CHORUS

If those young girls are taken away from here,
I will not let you leave.

CREON

If you do that,
you'll soon be giving Thebes a greater prize—
for I'll be taking more than these two girls.

CHORUS

What do you mean to do?

CREON *[pointing to Oedipus]*

I'll seize that man
and carry him away.

CHORUS

That's a bold threat.

CREON

One that will be made good without delay,
unless this country's ruler intervenes.

OEDIPUS

You glib talker! Would you lay hands on me?

ΚΡΕΩΝ

αὐδῶ σιωπᾶν.

ΟΙΔΙΠΟΥΣ

μὴ γὰρ αἵδε δαίμονες
θεῖέν μ' ἄφωνον τῆσδε τῆς ἀρᾶς ἔτι,
ὅς μ', ὦ κάκιστε, ψιλὸν ὄμμ' ἀποσπάσας
πρὸς ὄμμασιν τοῖς πρόσθεν ἐξοίχει βίᾳ.
τοιγὰρ σέ τ' αὐτὸν καὶ γένος τὸ σὸν θεῶν
ὁ πάντα λεύσσων Ἥλιος δοίη βίον
τοιοῦτον οἷον κἀμὲ γηρᾶναί ποτε.

ΚΡΕΩΝ

ὁρᾶτε ταῦτα, τῆσδε γῆς ἐγχώριοι;

ΟΙΔΙΠΟΥΣ

ὁρῶσι κἀμὲ καὶ σέ, καὶ φρονοῦσ' ὅτι
ἔργοις πεπονθὼς ῥήμασίν σ' ἀμύνομαι.

ΚΡΕΩΝ

οὔτοι καθέξω θυμόν, ἀλλ' ἄξω βίᾳ
κεἰ μοῦνός εἰμι τόνδε καὶ χρόνῳ βραδύς.

ΟΙΔΙΠΟΥΣ

ἰὼ τάλας.

ΧΟΡΟΣ

ὅσον λῆμ' ἔχων ἀφίκου, ξέν', εἰ τάδε δοκεῖς τελεῖν.

ΚΡΕΩΝ

δοκῶ.

ΧΟΡΟΣ

τάνδ' ἄρ' οὐκέτι νεμῶ πόλιν.

ΚΡΕΩΝ

τοῖς τοι δικαίοις χὠ βραχὺς νικᾷ μέγαν.

ΟΙΔΙΠΟΥΣ

ἀκούεθ' οἷα φθέγγεται;

CREON
Do as I tell you and keep quiet!

OEDIPUS
No!
May the spirits here permit me to call down
one more curse against you, you worst of men,
since you have hauled away that helpless girl
and taken by force my one remaining eye.
May all-seeing Helios, god of the sun,
grant you and your entire family
a life like mine when you are growing old.

CREON
Do you see this, you men of Colonus?

OEDIPUS
They are observing you and me—they see
that when hostile actions make me suffer,
I defend myself with words.

CREON
I'll not check
the anger in my heart one moment more—
though I'm alone and age has slowed me down,
I'll seize this man and lead him off by force!

[CREON moves to take OEDIPUS away by himself.]

OEDIPUS *[struggling with Creon]*
Help me! Help!

CHORUS
How insolent you are, stranger,
if you believe you can accomplish this!

CREON
That is my intention.

CHORUS
If you succeed,
then I will say our city is no more.

CREON
With justice on its side, weakness conquers might.

OEDIPUS *[still struggling with Creon]*
You hear the sort of words he splutters?

ΧΟΡΟΣ

τά γ' οὐ τελεῖ.
[ἴστω μέγας Ζεύς.]

ΚΡΕΩΝ

Ζεύς γ' ἂν εἰδείη, σὺ δ' οὔ.

ΧΟΡΟΣ

ἆρ' οὐχ ὕβρις τάδ';

ΚΡΕΩΝ

ὕβρις, ἀλλ' ἀνεκτέα.

ΧΟΡΟΣ

ἰὼ πᾶς λεώς, ἰὼ γᾶς πρόμοι,
μόλετε σὺν τάχει, μόλετ', ἐπεὶ πέραν περῶσ'
οἵδε δή.

ΘΗΣΕΥΣ

τίς ποθ' ἡ βοή; τί τοὔργον; ἐκ τίνος φόβου ποτὲ
βουθυτοῦντά μ' ἀμφὶ βωμὸν ἔσχετ' ἐναλίῳ θεῷ
τοῦδ' ἐπιστάτῃ Κολωνοῦ; λέξαθ', ὡς εἰδῶ τὸ πᾶν,
οὗ χάριν δεῦρ' ᾖξα θᾶσσον ἢ καθ' ἡδονὴν ποδός.

ΟΙΔΙΠΟΥΣ

ὦ φίλτατ', ἔγνων γὰρ τὸ προσφώνημά σου,
πέπονθα δεινὰ τοῦδ' ὑπ' ἀνδρὸς ἀρτίως.

ΘΗΣΕΥΣ

τὰ ποῖα ταῦτα, τίς δ' ὁ πημήνας; λέγε.

ΟΙΔΙΠΟΥΣ

Κρέων ὅδ', ὃν δέδορκας, οἴχεται τέκνων
ἀποσπάσας μου τὴν μόνην ξυνωρίδα.

ΘΗΣΕΥΣ

πῶς εἶπας;

CHORUS

But great Zeus knows that he will not succeed
in doing what he says.

CREON

Zeus may well know,
but you do not.

CHORUS

Your actions are outrageous!

CREON

An outrage? Yes, but one you must endure!

CHORUS

All those of you who rule this land, help! Help!
Come here on the run! Come on! These Thebans
are on the move back across the border!

[THESEUS enters with a few ATTENDANTS]

THESEUS

Why all this shouting? What's happening here?
What are you afraid of? Why did you stop
my sacrifice at the altar to Poseidon,
god of the sea and lord of Colonus?
Explain all this so that I understand
why I had to hurry here more quickly
than was convenient.

OEDIPUS

I know that voice!
My dearest friend, I have just been suffering
dreadful things from this creature here.

THESEUS

What things?
Who has mistreated you? Tell me.

OEDIPUS

Creon has—
the man you see here. He took my children,
the only two I have.

THESEUS

What are you saying?

Οιδιπους

οἷά περ πέπονθ' ἀκήκοας.

Θησευς

οὔκουν τις ὡς τάχιστα προσπόλων μολὼν
πρὸς τούσδε βωμούς, πάντ' ἀναγκάσει λεὼν
ἄνιππον ἱππότην τε θυμάτων ἄπο
σπεύδειν ἀπὸ ῥυτῆρος, ἔνθα δίστομοι
μάλιστα συμβάλλουσιν ἐμπόρων ὁδοί,
ὡς μὴ παρέλθωσ' αἱ κόραι, γέλως δ' ἐγὼ
ξένῳ γένωμαι τῷδε, χειρωθεὶς βίᾳ.
ἴθ', ὡς ἄνωγα, σὺν τάχει. τοῦτον δ' ἐγώ,
εἰ μὲν δι' ὀργῆς ἧκον, ἧς ὅδ' ἄξιος,
ἄτρωτον οὐ μεθῆκ' ἂν ἐξ ἐμῆς χερός.
νῦν δ' οὕσπερ αὐτὸς τοὺς νόμους εἰσῆλθ' ἔχων,
τούτοισι κοὐκ ἄλλοισιν ἁρμοσθήσεται.
οὐ γάρ ποτ' ἔξει τῆσδε τῆς χώρας, πρὶν ἂν
κείνας ἐναργεῖς δεῦρό μοι στήσῃς ἄγων·
ἐπεὶ δέδρακας οὔτ' ἐμοῦ καταξίως
οὔθ' ὧν πέφυκας αὐτὸς οὔτε σῆς χθονός·
ὅστις δίκαι' ἀσκοῦσαν εἰσελθὼν πόλιν
κἄνευ νόμου κραίνουσαν οὐδέν, εἶτ' ἀφεὶς
τὰ τῆσδε τῆς γῆς κύρι', ὧδ' ἐπεισπεσὼν
ἄγεις θ' ἃ χρῄζεις καὶ παρίστασαι βίᾳ,
καί μοι πόλιν κένανδρον ἢ δούλην τινὰ
ἔδοξας εἶναι κἄμ' ἴσον τῷ μηδενί.
καίτοι σε Θῆβαί γ' οὐκ ἐπαίδευσαν κακόν·
οὐ γὰρ φιλοῦσιν ἄνδρας ἐκδίκους τρέφειν,
οὐδ' ἄν σ' ἐπαινέσειαν, εἰ πυθοίατο
συλῶντα τἀμὰ καὶ τὰ τῶν θεῶν, βίᾳ
ἄγοντα φωτῶν ἀθλίων ἱκτήρια.
οὔκουν ἔγωγ' ἂν σῆς ἐπεμβαίνων χθονός,
οὐδ' εἰ τὰ πάντων εἶχον ἐνδικώτατα,
ἄνευ γε τοῦ κραίνοντος, ὅστις ἦν, χθονὸς
οὔθ' εἷλκον οὔτ' ἂν ἦγον, ἀλλ' ἠπιστάμην

OEDIPUS
I've told you what I have had to suffer.

THESEUS *[to his ATTENDANTS]*
One of you men, go as fast as you can
to those altars. Tell all the people there
to leave the sacrifice and move full speed—
both on foot and horseback—to that junction
where two highroads meet, so those young girls
do not pass by the place and I become
an object to be laughed at by this stranger
because his power got the better of me.
Go now! Do as I say—and quickly!

[One of the attendants accompanying Theseus runs off. THESEUS turns his attention to CREON]

As for this man, if my anger judged him
as he deserves, he would not escape my hand
without some injury. But now those laws
he himself brought with him when he came here
will render judgment—we need no others.
You will not leave this land until you bring
those young girls back and set them in plain view
right here in front of me. What you have done
is a disgrace to me, to your parents,
and to your native land. You marched in here,
to a city state that honours justice
and never condones acts outside the law,
and brushed aside this land's authorities,
bursting in like this and seizing prisoners,
using force to take whatever you desired.
You seem to think this city has no men
or is full of slaves and I am nothing.
It was not Thebes who taught you to be bad.
That state does not like raising lawless men
and would not praise your actions if it learned
that you were stealing from me and the gods,
forcefully abducting their poor suppliants.
If I were to move into your country,
even with the most righteous of all claims,
I would not seize someone or lead them off
without permission of the ruling power,
whoever he might be. I would know how

ξένον παρ' ἀστοῖς ὡς διαιτᾶσθαι χρεών.
σὺ δ' ἀξίαν οὐκ οὖσαν αἰσχύνεις πόλιν
τὴν αὐτὸς αὑτοῦ, καί σ' ὁ πληθύων χρόνος
γέρονθ' ὁμοῦ τίθησι καὶ τοῦ νοῦ κενόν.
εἶπον μὲν οὖν καὶ πρόσθεν, ἐννέπω δὲ νῦν,
τὰς παῖδας ὡς τάχιστα δεῦρ' ἄγειν τινά,
εἰ μὴ μέτοικος τῆσδε τῆς χώρας θέλεις
εἶναι βίᾳ τε κοὐχ ἑκών· καὶ ταῦτά σοι
τῷ νῷ θ' ὁμοίως κἀπὸ τῆς γλώσσης λέγω.

Χορος

ὁρᾷς ἵν' ἥκεις, ὦ ξέν'; ὡς ἀφ' ὧν μὲν εἶ
φαίνει δίκαιος, δρῶν δ' ἐφευρίσκει κακά.

Κρεων

ἐγὼ οὔτ' ἄνανδρον τήνδε τὴν πόλιν νέμων,
ὦ τέκνον Αἰγέως, οὔτ' ἄβουλον, ὡς σὺ φῄς,
τοὔργον τόδ' ἐξέπραξα, γιγνώσκων δ' ὅτι
οὐδείς ποτ' αὐτοὺς τῶν ἐμῶν ἂν ἐμπέσοι
ζῆλος ξυναίμων, ὥστ' ἐμοῦ τρέφειν βίᾳ.
ᾔδη δ' ὁθούνεκ' ἄνδρα καὶ πατροκτόνον
κἄναγνον οὐ δεξοίατ', οὐδ' ὅτῳ γάμοι
ξυνόντες ηὑρέθησαν ἀνόσιοι τέκνων.
τοιοῦτον αὐτοῖς Ἄρεος εὔβουλον πάγον
ἐγὼ ξυνῄδη χθόνιον ὄνθ', ὃς οὐκ ἐᾷ
τοιούσδ' ἀλήτας τῇδ' ὁμοῦ ναίειν πόλει·
ᾧ πίστιν ἴσχων τήνδ' ἐχειρούμην ἄγραν.
καὶ ταῦτ' ἂν οὐκ ἔπρασσον, εἰ μή μοι πικρὰς
αὐτῷ τ' ἀρὰς ἠρᾶτο καὶ τὠμῷ γένει·
ἀνθ' ὧν πεπονθὼς ἠξίουν τάδ' ἀντιδρᾶν.
θυμοῦ γὰρ οὐδὲν γῆράς ἐστιν ἄλλο πλὴν
θανεῖν· θανόντων δ' οὐδὲν ἄλγος ἅπτεται.
πρὸς ταῦτα πράξεις οἷον ἂν θέλῃς· ἐπεὶ
ἐρημία με, κεἰ δίκαι', ὅμως λέγω,
σμικρὸν τίθησι· πρὸς δὲ τὰς πράξεις ὅμως,
καὶ τηλικόσδ' ὤν, ἀντιδρᾶν πειράσομαι.

a stranger ought to act with citizens.
But you are a disgrace to your own city.
Thebes does not deserve that. Advancing years
have made you old and robbed you of all sense.
So I tell you now what I said before—
have those girls brought here as quickly as you can,
unless you wish to be held here by force,
a resident of this land against your will.
What my tongue utters, I intend to do.

CHORUS *[to Creon]*
You see the situation you are in, stranger?
From your origins you seem a righteous man,
but your actions show you are dishonest.

CREON
Son of Aegeus, I have not done these things
because I thought Athens was devoid of men,
as you have claimed. No. I had sound reasons.
But I did not believe your citizens
would be so devoted to my relatives
that they would keep them here against my will.
And I was sure people would not welcome
a polluted man, who killed his father
and whose unholy marriage was exposed,
a mother wedded to her son. For I knew
such wise restrictions were traditional
with the Council on the Hill of Ares,
which never would permit such vagrant types
to settle in the Athenian state.[37]
Trusting that knowledge, I chased down my prey.
But I would not have acted in this fashion,
if he had not called down stinging curses
on my family and me. In my view,
what he made me suffer entitled me
to take revenge. Anger never grows old
until death comes, for dead men feel no pain.
You will deal with this however you wish.
What I say is right, but I am alone
and therefore feeble. Still, though I am old,
I will seek to pay you back for what you do.

ΟΙΔΙΠΟΥΣ

ὦ λῆμ᾽ ἀναιδές, τοῦ καθυβρίζειν δοκεῖς,
πότερον ἐμοῦ γέροντος ἢ σαυτοῦ, τόδε;
ὅστις φόνους μοι καὶ γάμους καὶ συμφορὰς
τοῦ σοῦ διῆκας στόματος, ἃς ἐγὼ τάλας
ἤνεγκον ἄκων· θεοῖς γὰρ ἦν οὕτω φίλον,
τάχ᾽ ἄν τι μηνίουσιν εἰς γένος πάλαι.
ἐπεὶ καθ᾽ αὑτόν γ᾽ οὐκ ἂν ἐξεύροις ἐμοὶ
ἁμαρτίας ὄνειδος οὐδέν, ἀνθ᾽ ὅτου
τάδ᾽ εἰς ἐμαυτὸν τοὺς ἐμούς θ᾽ ἡμάρτανον.
ἐπεὶ δίδαξον, εἴ τι θέσφατον πατρὶ
χρησμοῖσιν ἱκνεῖθ᾽ ὥστε πρὸς παίδων θανεῖν,
πῶς ἂν δικαίως τοῦτ᾽ ὀνειδίζοις ἐμοί,
ὃς οὔτε βλάστας πω γενεθλίους πατρός,
οὐ μητρὸς εἶχον, ἀλλ᾽ ἀγέννητος τότ᾽ ἦ;
εἰ δ᾽ αὖ φανεὶς δύστηνος, ὡς ἐγὼ ᾽φάνην,
ἐς χεῖρας ἦλθον πατρὶ καὶ κατέκτανον,
μηδὲν ξυνιεὶς ὧν ἔδρων εἰς οὕς τ᾽ ἔδρων,
πῶς ἂν τό γ᾽ ἆκον πρᾶγμ᾽ ἂν εἰκότως ψέγοις;
μητρὸς δέ, τλῆμον, οὐκ ἐπαισχύνει γάμους
οὔσης ὁμαίμου σῆς μ᾽ ἀναγκάζων λέγειν,
οἵους ἐρῶ τάχ᾽· οὐ γὰρ οὖν σιγήσομαι,
σοῦ γ᾽ εἰς τόδ᾽ ἐξελθόντος ἀνόσιον στόμα.
ἔτικτε γάρ μ᾽ ἔτικτεν, ὤμοι μοι κακῶν,
οὐκ εἰδότ᾽ οὐκ εἰδυῖα, καὶ τεκοῦσά με,
αὑτῆς ὄνειδος παῖδας ἐξέφυσέ μοι.
ἀλλ᾽ ἓν γὰρ οὖν ἔξοιδα, σὲ μὲν ἑκόντ᾽ ἐμὲ
κείνην τε ταῦτα δυσστομεῖν· ἐγὼ δέ νιν
ἄκων ἔγημα φθέγγομαί τ᾽ ἄκων τάδε.
ἀλλ᾽ οὐ γὰρ οὔτ᾽ ἐν τοῖσδ᾽ ἁλώσομαι κακὸς
γάμοισιν οὔθ᾽ οὓς αἰὲν ἐμφορεῖς σύ μοι
φόνους πατρῴους ἐξονειδίζων πικρῶς.

Oedipus

What blatant arrogance! For whose old age
do you think this abuse is more degrading,
yours or mine? Against me that mouth of yours
spits out words like murder, incest, misery—
sufferings I, in my wretchedness, endured
through no fault of my own. All these events
were pleasing to the gods—perhaps because
my family long ago offended them.
For looking at my life, you could not find
a single reason to blame me for mistakes
for which I needed to pay retribution
with destructive acts injuring myself
and my own kindred. Explain this to me:
if some divine voice in an oracle
told my father he was going to die
at the hand of his own son, how can you
justly blame me for it. I was not born.
No father's seed had yet begotten me,
nor had any mother's womb conceived me.
I did not exist! And if I was born,
as I was, to a life of wretchedness,
had a lethal fight with my own father,
and killed him, with no idea who he was
or what I had done, are you justified
in disparaging me for what I did
without intending to? As for my mother,
you disgraceful brute, are you not ashamed
to force me to speak about her marriage,
when she was your sister? Well then, I shall.
I will not stay silent about the details,
when you have gone to such great lengths to talk
of sacrilegious things. She gave birth to me—
yes, alas for me, she was my mother.
But I did not know that, and nor did she.
And she had children with the son she bore,
to her great shame. But this one thing I know—
you freely choose to heap insults on us,
but I did not freely choose to marry her,
nor do I ever choose to mention it.
No, I will not be called an evil man
because I married her and killed my father,
that death you keep on hurling in my teeth,
always abusing me with bitter insults.

ἓν γάρ μ' ἄμειψαι μοῦνον ὧν σ' ἀνιστορῶ.
εἴ τις σὲ τὸν δίκαιον αὐτίκ' ἐνθάδε
κτείνοι παραστάς, πότερα πυνθάνοι' ἂν εἰ
πατήρ σ' ὁ καίνων ἢ τίνοι' ἂν εὐθέως;
δοκῶ μέν, εἴπερ ζῆν φιλεῖς, τὸν αἴτιον
τίνοι' ἂν οὐδὲ τοὔνδικον περιβλέποις.
τοιαῦτα μέντοι καὐτὸς εἰσέβην κακά,
θεῶν ἀγόντων· οἷς ἐγὼ οὐδὲ τὴν πατρὸς
ψυχὴν ἂν οἶμαι ζῶσαν ἀντειπεῖν ἐμοί.
σὺ δ', εἶ γὰρ οὐ δίκαιος, ἀλλ' ἅπαν καλὸν
λέγειν νομίζων ῥητὸν ἄρρητόν τ' ἔπος,
τοιαῦτ' ὀνειδίζεις με τῶνδ' ἐναντίον.
καί σοι τὸ Θησέως ὄνομα θωπεῦσαι καλόν,
καὶ τὰς Ἀθήνας, ὡς κατῴκηνται καλῶς·
κᾆθ' ὧδ' ἐπαινῶν πολλὰ τοῦδ' ἐκλανθάνει,
ὁθούνεκ' εἴ τις γῆ θεοὺς ἐπίσταται
τιμαῖς σεβίζειν, ἥδε τοῦθ' ὑπερφέρει·
ἀφ' ἧς σὺ κλέψας τὸν ἱκέτην γέροντ' ἐμὲ
αὐτόν τ' ἐχειροῦ τὰς κόρας τ' οἴχει λαβών.
ἀνθ' ὧν ἐγὼ νῦν τάσδε τὰς θεὰς ἐμοὶ
καλῶν ἱκνοῦμαι καὶ κατασκήπτω λιταῖς
ἐλθεῖν ἀρωγοὺς ξυμμάχους θ', ἵν' ἐκμάθῃς
οἵων ὑπ' ἀνδρῶν ἥδε φρουρεῖται πόλις.

Χορος

ὁ ξεῖνος, ὦναξ, χρηστός· αἱ δὲ συμφοραὶ
αὐτοῦ πανώλεις, ἄξιαι δ' ἀμυναθεῖν.

Θησευς

ἅλις λόγων, ὡς οἱ μὲν ἐξειργασμένοι
σπεύδουσιν, ἡμεῖς δ' οἱ παθόντες ἕσταμεν.

Here is a question. How would you answer?
If someone were to march in here right now
and attempt to kill you, you righteous man,
would your first response be to ask the killer,
"Are you my father?" or to fight him back?
It seems to me that, if you love your life,
you would fight back against the murderer,
not search for what was legally correct.
That is how I was led on by the gods
and embarked upon a life of evils.
I do not think my father's ghostly shade,
if it came back to life, would contradict me.
But because you are not a righteous man,
you think you can say anything at all,
without considering if what you speak
is suitable or should not be mentioned.
And so in front of all these people here
you keep hurling accusations at me.
You think it serves your purposes to flatter
the great name of Theseus and Athens
as a well-governed state. But when you praise,
you forget that if there is one city
that understands how to respect the gods
that place is Athens—she excels in that.
Yet it is from here you wished to steal me,
an old man and a suppliant, as well.
You laid hands on me, tried to drag me off,
after having hauled away my daughters.
So now I call upon these goddesses,
I appeal to them, and with my prayers
I beseech them to come to my aid here,
to fight on my behalf, so you may learn
the quality of those who guard this city.

Chorus

My lord, this stranger is a worthy man.
His misfortunes have been devastating,
but he deserves our help.

Theseus

We have talked enough!
Those who took the girls are hurrying off,
while we, the ones they robbed, are standing still.

ΚΡΕΩΝ

τί δῆτ᾽ ἀμαυρῷ φωτὶ προστάσσεις ποεῖν;

ΘΗΣΕΥΣ

ὁδοῦ κατάρχειν τῆς ἐκεῖ, πομπὸν δέ με
χωρεῖν, ἵν᾽, εἰ μὲν ἐν τόποισι τοῖσδ᾽ ἔχεις
τὰς παῖδας ἡμῖν αὐτὸς ἐκδείξῃς ἐμοί·
εἰ δ᾽ ἐγκρατεῖς φεύγουσιν, οὐδὲν δεῖ πονεῖν.
ἄλλοι γὰρ οἱ σπεύδοντες, οὓς οὐ μή ποτε
χώρας φυγόντες τῆσδ᾽ ἐπεύξωνται θεοῖς.
ἀλλ᾽ ἐξυφηγοῦ· γνῶθι δ᾽ ὡς ἔχων ἔχει
καί σ᾽ εἷλε θηρῶνθ᾽ ἡ τύχη· τὰ γὰρ δόλῳ
τῷ μὴ δικαίῳ κτήματ᾽ οὐχὶ σῴζεται.
κοὐκ ἄλλον ἕξεις εἰς τάδ᾽· ὡς ἔξοιδά σε
οὐ ψιλὸν οὐδ᾽ ἄσκευον ἐς τοσήνδ᾽ ὕβριν
ἥκοντα τόλμης τῆς παρεστώσης τανῦν,
ἀλλ᾽ ἔσθ᾽ ὅτῳ σὺ πιστὸς ὢν ἔδρας τάδε.
ἃ δεῖ μ᾽ ἀθρῆσαι, μηδὲ τήνδε τὴν πόλιν
ἑνὸς ποῆσαι φωτὸς ἀσθενεστέραν.
νοεῖς τι τούτων, ἢ μάτην τὰ νῦν τέ σοι
δοκεῖ λελέχθαι χὤτε ταῦτ᾽ ἐμηχανῶ;

ΚΡΕΩΝ

οὐδὲν σὺ μεμπτὸν ἐνθάδ᾽ ὢν ἐρεῖς ἐμοί·
οἴκοι δὲ χἠμεῖς εἰσόμεσθ᾽ ἃ χρὴ ποεῖν.

ΘΗΣΕΥΣ

χωρῶν ἀπείλει νῦν· σὺ δ᾽ ἡμίν, Οἰδίπους,
ἕκηλος αὐτοῦ μίμνε, πιστωθεὶς ὅτι,
ἢν μὴ θάνω ᾽γὼ πρόσθεν, οὐχὶ παύσομαι
πρὶν ἄν σε τῶν σῶν κύριον στήσω τέκνων.

CREON

I am a weak man. What would you have me do?

THESEUS

I want you to lead us on the pathway
to those girls, while I serve as your escort,
so if you are keeping those two children
in this place, you will personally show me
where they are. But if those who have seized them
are on the run, there is nothing we need do,
for other men are chasing after them,
from whom they never will escape and leave
this land to give thank offerings to the gods.
Come, then, lead on. And you might ponder this—
the hunter has been hunted down, and Fate
has seized you while you were stalking others.
What people gain unjustly with a trick
they do not keep, and no one else involved
will help you in this matter. For I know
you would not reach such heights of insolence
and act so recklessly as you do now
all on your own, without accomplices.
You were relying on someone else's help
when you resolved to carry out this act.[38]
I need to think further on this matter—
one man must not prove stronger than the state.
Do these words of warning make any sense,
or do they now seem as meaningless to you
as what you heard when you were planning this?

CREON

Here in Athens, you can say what you wish.
I will not object. But when I am home,
I, too, will realize what must be done.

THESEUS

Make your threats, but move. And you, Oedipus,
stay here, and do not worry. Trust this pledge—
unless I die beforehand, I will not rest
until I have restored your children to you.

[CREON, THESEUS, and the ATTENDANTS leave]

Οιδιπογς

ὄναιο, Θησεῦ, τοῦ τε γενναίου χάριν
καὶ τῆς πρὸς ἡμᾶς ἐνδίκου προμηθίας.

Χορος

εἴην ὅθι δαΐων
ἀνδρῶν τάχ' ἐπιστροφαὶ
τὸν χαλκοβόαν Ἄρη
μείξουσιν, ἢ πρὸς Πυθίαις
ἢ λαμπάσιν ἀκταῖς,
οὗ πότνιαι σεμνὰ τιθηνοῦνται τέλη
θνατοῖσιν, ὧν καὶ χρυσέα
κλῂς ἐπὶ γλώσσᾳ βέβακε
προσπόλων Εὐμολπιδᾶν·
ἔνθ' οἶμαι τὸν ἐγρεμάχαν
Θησέα καὶ τὰς διστόλους
ἀδμῆτας ἀδελφὰς
αὐτάρκει τάχ' ἐμμίξειν βοᾷ
τούσδ' ἀνὰ χώρους·

ἤ που τὸν ἐφεσπέρου
πέτρας νιφάδος πελῶσ'
Οἰάτιδος εἰς νόμον,
πώλοισιν ἢ ῥιμφαρμάτοις
φεύγοντες ἁμίλλαις.
ἁλώσεται· δεινὸς ὁ προσχώρων Ἄρης,
δεινὰ δὲ Θησειδᾶν ἀκμά.
πᾶς γὰρ ἀστράπτει χαλινός,
πᾶσα δ' ὁρμᾶται καθεῖσ'
ἀμπυκτήρια στομίων
ἄμβασις, οἳ τὰν ἱππίαν
τιμῶσιν Ἀθάναν
καὶ τὸν πόντιον γαιάοχον
Ῥέας φίλον υἱόν.

ἔρδουσ' ἢ μέλλουσιν; ὡς
προμνᾶταί τί μοι
γνώμα τάχ' ἀντάσειν
τᾶν δεινὰ τλασᾶν, δεινὰ δ' εὑρουσᾶν πρὸς αὐθαίμων πάθη.

Oedipus *[calling after Theseus]*
Bless you, Theseus, for your noble heart
and for your righteous care on my behalf!

Chorus
O how I wish I could be there,
where the enemy wheels to fight
and quickly joins the battle clash,
the clamour of Ares' brazen spears,
hard by the Phythian shore—
or else beside the torch-lit strand
where those two goddesses perform
their sacred rites for mortal men
whose tongues their holy ministers,
the Eumolpidae, have silenced
by placing there a seal of gold.[39]
There, I think, our warlike Theseus
and those two unmarried girls
will soon meet in this land of ours,
amid the cries of our brave fighting men.

Or else they may be closing in
on pastures west of Oea's snowy peak,
racing ahead on youthful horses,
their chariots careening at full speed.
Now Creon will be overthrown!
Our men are terrifying in war,
and Theseus' troops are battle strong.
Every bit and bridle glitters,
as all our horsemen charge the foe,
in honour of equestrian Athena
and the god encircling the earth,
lord of the sea, Rhea's beloved son.[40]

Have they already come to blows,
or are our men about to fight?
My mind is telling me to hope
we soon will meet those two young girls,
whose suffering has been intense,
afflictions they have undergone
at the blood-linked hands of their own kin.

τελεῖ τελεῖ Ζεύς τι κατ᾽ ἆμαρ
μάντις εἴμ᾽ ἐσθλῶν ἀγώνων.
εἴθ᾽ ἀελλαία ταχύρρωστος πελειὰς
αἰθερίας νεφέλας κύρσαιμ᾽ ἄνωθ᾽ ἀγώνων
αἰωρήσασα τοὐμὸν ὄμμα.

ἰὼ θεῶν πάνταρχε, παντ-
όπτα Ζεῦ, πόροις
γᾶς τᾶσδε δαμούχοις
σθένει ᾽πινικείῳ τὸν εὔαγρον τελειῶσαι λόχον,
σεμνά τε παῖς Παλλὰς Ἀθάνα.
καὶ τὸν ἀγρευτὰν Ἀπόλλω
καὶ κασιγνήταν πυκνοστίκτων ὀπαδὸν
ὠκυπόδων ἐλάφων στέργω διπλᾶς ἀρωγὰς
μολεῖν γᾷ τᾷδε καὶ πολίταις.

— ὦ ξεῖν᾽ ἀλῆτα, τῷ σκοπῷ μὲν οὐκ ἐρεῖς
ὡς ψευδόμαντις· τὰς κόρας γὰρ εἰσορῶ
τάσδ᾽ ἆσσον αὖθις ὧδε προσπολουμένας.

Οιδιπουσ

ποῦ ποῦ; τί φής; πῶς εἶπας;

Αντιγονη

ὦ πάτερ πάτερ,
τίς ἂν θεῶν σοι τόνδ᾽ ἄριστον ἄνδρ᾽ ἰδεῖν
δοίη, τὸν ἡμᾶς δεῦρο προσπέμψαντά σοι;

Οιδιπουσ

ὦ τέκνον, ἦ πάρεστον;

Αντιγονη

αἵδε γὰρ χέρες
Θησέως ἔσωσαν φιλτάτων τ᾽ ὀπαόνων.

Today Zeus brings some great event
to its fulfilment, its final end.
I can foresee a glorious fight!
O to be a dove on the wing,
as strong and swift as a storming wind,
to soar up high in the upper air
and gaze from a cloud on the battle below!

O Zeus, who watches everything,
almighty king of all the gods,
grant to defenders of this land
the strength to win a victory,
to catch the enemy unaware
and end the chase successfully!
And I pray that Pallas Athena
your revered daughter, grants that, too,
as well as Apollo, the hunter god,
and with him his sister Artemis,
who tracks swift-moving speckled deer—
O may they bring their two-fold help,
assisting our citizens and Athens.

[Enter THESEUS, ANTIGONE, ISMENE, and ATTENDANTS]

CHORUS *[to OEDIPUS]*
Well, my wandering friend, you cannot say
those watching out for you are lying prophets—
I see your daughters being escorted back.

OEDIPUS
What? Where are they? What are you talking about?

ANTIGONE
O father, father, I wish one of the gods
would let you see this very best of men,
who brought us here and led us back to y0u.

OEDIPUS
My child, are you really here, both of you?

ANTIGONE
Yes—saved by the strong hands of Theseus
and his most loyal comrades.

ΟΙΔΙΠΟΥΣ

προσέλθετ' ὦ παῖ, πατρὶ καὶ τὸ μηδαμὰ
ἐλπισθὲν ἥξειν σῶμα βαστάσαι δότε.

ΑΝΤΙΓΟΝΗ

αἰτεῖς ἃ τεύξει· σὺν πόθῳ γὰρ ἡ χάρις.

ΟΙΔΙΠΟΥΣ

ποῦ δῆτα, ποῦ 'στόν;

ΑΝΤΙΓΟΝΗ

αἵδ' ὁμοῦ πελάζομεν.

ΟΙΔΙΠΟΥΣ

ὦ φίλτατ' ἔρνη.

ΑΝΤΙΓΟΝΗ

τῷ τεκόντι πᾶν φίλον.

ΟΙΔΙΠΟΥΣ

ὦ σκῆπτρα φωτός.

ΑΝΤΙΓΟΝΗ

δυσμόρου γε δύσμορα.

ΟΙΔΙΠΟΥΣ

ἔχω τὰ φίλτατ', οὐδ' ἔτ' ἂν πανάθλιος
θανὼν ἂν εἴην σφῷν παρεστώσαιν ἐμοί.
ἐρείσατ', ὦ παῖ, πλευρὸν ἀμφιδέξιον
ἐμφύντε τῷ φύσαντι, κἀναπαύσατον
τοῦ πρόσθ' ἐρήμου τοῦδε δυστήνου πλάνου.
καί μοι τὰ πραχθέντ' εἴπαθ' ὡς βράχιστ', ἐπεὶ
ταῖς τηλικαῖσδε σμικρὸς ἐξαρκεῖ λόγος.

ΑΝΤΙΓΟΝΗ

ὅδ' ἔσθ' ὁ σώσας· τοῦδε χρὴ κλύειν, πάτερ,
οὗ κἄστι τοὔργον· τοὐμὸν ὧδ' ἔσται βραχύ.

OEDIPUS

O children,
come to your father and let me hold you.
I was losing hope you would be coming back.

ANTIGONE

You will get your wish. That embrace you want
is what we long for.

OEDIPUS

Where are the two of you?

ANTIGONE

We're coming—both of us together.

[ANTIGONE, ISMENE, and OEDIPUS embrace]

OEDIPUS

My dearest children!

ANTIGONE

To any father
every child is dear.

OEDIPUS

An old man's support . . .

ANTIGONE

With a destiny as wretched as his own.

OEDIPUS

I am now holding those I love the most.
If I should die with you two beside me,
I could not be entirely unhappy.
O children, hold me close—one on each side—
cling to your father, help him recover
from his past days of lonely wandering,
a life of misery. And now tell us
what you went through, but keep the speeches short—
from girls like you a brief word is enough.

ANTIGONE

Father, the one who rescued us is here.
He is the one you should be listening to,
the man who did it. What I have to say
will not be much.

ΟΙΔΙΠΟΥΣ

ὦ ξεῖνε, μὴ θαύμαζε, πρὸς τὸ λιπαρὲς
τέκν᾽ εἰ φανέντ᾽ ἄελπτα μηκύνω λόγον.
ἐπίσταμαι γὰρ τήνδε τὴν ἐς τάσδε μοι
τέρψιν παρ᾽ ἄλλου μηδενὸς πεφασμένην·
σὺ γάρ νιν ἐξέσωσας, οὐκ ἄλλος βροτῶν.
καί σοι θεοὶ πόροιεν ὡς ἐγὼ θέλω,
αὐτῷ τε καὶ γῇ τῇδ᾽, ἐπεὶ τό γ᾽ εὐσεβὲς
μόνοις παρ᾽ ὑμῖν ηὗρον ἀνθρώπων ἐγὼ
καὶ τοὐπιεικὲς καὶ τὸ μὴ ψευδοστομεῖν.
εἰδὼς δ᾽ ἀμύνω τοῖσδε τοῖς λόγοις τάδε·
ἔχω γὰρ ἅχω διὰ σὲ κοὐκ ἄλλον βροτῶν·
καί μοι χέρ᾽, ὦναξ, δεξιὰν ὄρεξον, ὡς
ψαύσω φιλήσω τ᾽, εἰ θέμις, τὸ σὸν κάρα.
καίτοι τί φωνῶ; πῶς σ᾽ ἂν ἄθλιος γεγὼς
θιγεῖν θελήσαιμ᾽ ἀνδρός, ᾧ τίς οὐκ ἔνι
κηλὶς κακῶν ξύνοικος; οὐκ ἔγωγέ σε,
οὐδ᾽ οὖν ἐάσω· τοῖς γὰρ ἐμπείροις βροτῶν
μόνοις οἷόν τε συνταλαιπωρεῖν τάδε.
σὺ δ᾽ αὐτόθεν μοι χαῖρε καὶ τὰ λοιπά μου
μέλου δικαίως, ὥσπερ ἐς τόδ᾽ ἡμέρας.

ΘΗΣΕΥΣ

οὔτ᾽ εἴ τι μῆκος τῶν λόγων ἔθου πλέον,
τέκνοισι τερφθεὶς τοῖσδε, θαυμάσας ἔχω,
οὔτ᾽ εἰ πρὸ τοὐμοῦ προὔλαβες τὰ τῶνδ᾽ ἔπη.
βάρος γὰρ ἡμᾶς οὐδὲν ἐκ τούτων ἔχει.
οὐ γὰρ λόγοισι τὸν βίον σπουδάζομεν
λαμπρὸν ποεῖσθαι μᾶλλον ἢ τοῖς δρωμένοις.
δείκνυμι δ᾽· ὧν γὰρ ὤμοσ᾽ οὐκ ἐψευσάμην
οὐδέν σε, πρέσβυ· τάσδε γὰρ πάρειμ᾽ ἄγων
ζώσας, ἀκραιφνεῖς τῶν κατηπειλημένων.

OEDIPUS *[to THESEUS]*

You must not be amazed,
my friend, that I keep talking for so long
to these children, so suddenly restored.
For I know that my present joy in them
I owe entirely to you. You saved them—
you and no one else. And may gods grant
to you and to this land what I would wish,
for among all those living on the earth
only here with you have I encountered
men of piety and just character
who tell no lies. I know that about you,
and I pay tribute to your qualities
with these words of mine. Everything I have
I have because of you and no one else.
O royal king, hold your right hand out to me,
so I can touch it. If it is lawful,
let me be permitted to kiss your cheek.
But what am I saying? A wretch like me,
how could I want you to touch a man
in whom every form of defiling stain
has found a home? No, I will not touch you.
That is an action I cannot permit,
not even if you yourself were willing.
Only those mortals who have been with me
in my misfortunes can share my suffering.[41]
So from where you stand accept my gratitude,
and, as you have done up to this moment,
deal with me justly in the days to come.

THESEUS

Given your delight in these two children,
I am not surprised your conversation
has taken some time or that you prefer
to talk to them before you talk to me.
I can find no offence to me in that.
I do not wish to add lustre to my life
through the words I speak, but by what I do.
And I have demonstrated that to you,
old man, for my word has not proven false
in any of those promises I made.
I am here, having brought back your daughters
alive and unharmed by the threats they faced.

χὤπως μὲν ἁγὼν ᾑρέθη, τί δεῖ μάτην
κομπεῖν, ἅ γ' εἴσει καὐτὸς ἐκ ταύταιν ξυνών;
λόγος δ' ὃς ἐμπέπτωκεν ἀρτίως ἐμοὶ
στείχοντι δεῦρο, συμβαλοῦ γνώμην, ἐπεὶ
σμικρὸς μὲν εἰπεῖν, ἄξιος δὲ θαυμάσαι·
πρᾶγος δ' ἀτίζειν οὐδὲν ἄνθρωπον χρεών.

ΟΙΔΙΠΟΥΣ

τί δ' ἔστι, τέκνον Αἰγέως; δίδασκέ με
ὡς μὴ εἰδότ' αὐτὸν μηδὲν ὧν σὺ πυνθάνει.

ΘΗΣΕΥΣ

φασίν τιν' ἡμῖν ἄνδρα, σοὶ μὲν ἔμπολιν
οὐκ ὄντα, συγγενῆ δέ, προσπεσόντα πως
βωμῷ καθῆσθαι τῷ Ποσειδῶνος, παρ' ᾧ
θύων ἔκυρον, ἡνίχ' ὡρμώμην ἐγώ.

ΟΙΔΙΠΟΥΣ

ποδαπόν; τί προσχρῄζοντα τῷ θακήματι·

ΘΗΣΕΥΣ

οὐκ οἶδα πλὴν ἕν· σοῦ γάρ, ὡς λέγουσί μοι,
βραχύν τιν' αἰτεῖ μῦθον οὐκ ὄγκου πλέων.

ΟΙΔΙΠΟΥΣ

ποῖόν τιν'; οὐ γὰρ ἥδ' ἕδρα σμικροῦ λόγου.

ΘΗΣΕΥΣ

σοὶ φασὶν αὐτὸν ἐς λόγους ἐλθεῖν μόνον
αἰτεῖν ἀπελθεῖν τ' ἀσφαλῶς τῆς δεῦρ' ὁδοῦ.

ΟΙΔΙΠΟΥΣ

τίς δῆτ' ἂν εἴη τήνδ' ὁ προσθακῶν ἕδραν;

As for how we triumphed in that struggle,
why should I vainly boast about a fight
whose details you will hear from these two girls
when you get to spend some time together.
But a moment ago, on my way here,
I heard an odd report, and I would like
to learn what you advise. It was quite short,
but very strange and worth attending to,
for men should never overlook anything
that might be of concern.

OEDIPUS

What did it say,
son of Aegeus? Describe it to me.
Otherwise I have no idea at all
what you wish to know.

THESEUS

People say a man,
someone who is a relative of yours
but not from Thebes, has somehow made his way
to Poseidon's altar and is sitting there,
where I was offering a sacrifice
the first time I was summoned here.

OEDIPUS

Where is he from?
If he's a suppliant, what does he want?

THESEUS

From what people tell me, I only know
he wishes to have a brief word with you
about some minor matter.

OEDIPUS

What about?
If he's there sitting as a suppliant,
the issue is not trivial.

THESEUS

They say
he only wants to have a talk with you
and then safe passage to return from here.

OEDIPUS

Who would sit there praying for such things?

ΘΗΣΕΥΣ

ὅρα κατ᾽ Ἄργος εἴ τις ὑμὶν ἐγγενὴς
ἔσθ᾽, ὅστις ἄν σου τοῦτο προσχρῄζοι τυχεῖν.

ΟΙΔΙΠΟΥΣ

ὦ φίλτατε, σχὲς οὗπερ εἶ.

ΘΗΣΕΥΣ

τί δ᾽ ἔστι σοι;

ΟΙΔΙΠΟΥΣ

μή μου δεηθῇς.

ΘΗΣΕΥΣ

πράγματος ποίου; λέγε.

ΟΙΔΙΠΟΥΣ

ἔξοιδ᾽ ἀκούων τῶνδ᾽ ὅς ἐσθ᾽ ὁ προστάτης.

ΘΗΣΕΥΣ

καὶ τίς ποτ᾽ ἐστὶν ὅν γ᾽ ἐγὼ ψέξαιμί τι;

ΟΙΔΙΠΟΥΣ

παῖς οὑμός, ὦναξ, στυγνός, οὗ λόγων ἐγὼ
ἄλγιστ᾽ ἂν ἀνδρῶν ἐξανασχοίμην κλύων.

ΘΗΣΕΥΣ

τί δ᾽; οὐκ ἀκούειν ἔστι καὶ μὴ δρᾶν ἃ μὴ
χρῄζεις; τί σοι τοῦτ᾽ ἐστὶ λυπηρὸν κλύειν;

ΟΙΔΙΠΟΥΣ

ἔχθιστον, ὦναξ, φθέγμα τοῦθ᾽ ἥκει πατρί·
καὶ μή μ᾽ ἀνάγκῃ προσβάλῃς τάδ᾽ εἰκαθεῖν.

ΘΗΣΕΥΣ

ἀλλ᾽ εἰ τὸ θάκημ᾽ ἐξαναγκάζει, σκόπει
μή σοι πρόνοι᾽ ᾖ τοῦ θεοῦ φυλακτέα.

Theseus
Could it be a member of your family,
someone from Argos, who might be asking
a favour from you?

Oedipus
Stop there, my dear friend!

Theseus
What's troubling you?

Oedipus
You must not ask me to . . .

Theseus
Do what? Tell me.

Oedipus
From what you said just now,
I know the suppliant.

Theseus
Who is he?
And why should I find him offensive?

Oedipus
My lord, he is a son of mine, a person
I detest. What he has to say would pain me
more than words from any other man.

Theseus
What? Could you not just listen to him speak
and then not do what you don't wish to do?
Is there any harm in merely listening?

Oedipus
My lord, his voice has become abhorrent
to me, his father. Do not compel me
to yield to his request.

Theseus
But consider this—
does not the fact that he's a suppliant
force your hand? What about the reverence
you owe the god?

Αντιγονη

πάτερ, πιθοῦ μοι, κεἰ νέα παραινέσω.
τὸν ἄνδρ᾽ ἔασον τόνδε τῇ θ᾽ αὑτοῦ φρενὶ
χάριν παρασχεῖν τῷ θεῷ θ᾽ ἃ βούλεται,
καὶ νῷν ὕπεικε τὸν κασίγνητον μολεῖν.
οὐ γάρ σε, θάρσει, πρὸς βίαν παρασπάσει
γνώμης, ἃ μή σοι συμφέροντα λέξεται.
λόγων δ᾽ ἀκοῦσαι τίς βλάβη; τά τοι κακῶς
ηὑρημέν᾽ ἔργα τῷ λόγῳ μηνύεται.
ἔφυσας αὐτόν· ὥστε μηδὲ δρῶντά σε
τὰ τῶν κακίστων δυσσεβέστατ᾽, ὦ πάτερ,
θέμις σέ γ᾽ εἶναι κεῖνον ἀντιδρᾶν κακῶς.
ἀλλ᾽ ἔασον· εἰσὶ χἀτέροις γοναὶ κακαὶ
καὶ θυμὸς ὀξύς, ἀλλὰ νουθετούμενοι
φίλων ἐπῳδαῖς ἐξεπᾴδονται φύσιν.
σὺ δ᾽ εἰς ἐκεῖνα, μὴ τὰ νῦν, ἀποσκόπει
πατρῷα καὶ μητρῷα πήμαθ᾽ ἅπαθες·
κἂν κεῖνα λεύσσῃς, οἶδ᾽ ἐγώ, γνώσει κακοῦ
θυμοῦ τελευτὴν ὡς κακὴ προσγίγνεται.
ἔχεις γὰρ οὐχὶ βαιὰ τἀνθυμήματα,
τῶν σῶν ἀδέρκτων ὀμμάτων τητώμενος.
ἀλλ᾽ ἡμὶν εἶκε· λιπαρεῖν γὰρ οὐ καλὸν
δίκαια προσχρῄζουσιν, οὐδ᾽ αὐτὸν μὲν εὖ
πάσχειν, παθόντα δ᾽ οὐκ ἐπίστασθαι τίνειν.

Οιδιπους

τέκνον, βαρεῖαν ἡδονὴν νικᾶτέ με
λέγοντες· ἔστω δ᾽ οὖν ὅπως ὑμῖν φίλον.
μόνον, ξέν᾽, εἴπερ κεῖνος ὧδ᾽ ἐλεύσεται,
μηδεὶς κρατείτω τῆς ἐμῆς ψυχῆς ποτε.

ANTIGONE

Father, listen to me.
Though I am young, I'll offer my advice.
Permit the king to act as his own heart
and the god dictate and do what he desires.
And for the sake of your two daughters,
let our brother come here. You need not fear.
His words cannot force you to change your mind,
if what he says is not for your own good.
What harm is there in listening to him?
As you know, a conversation can expose
malicious acts someone intends to do.
Besides, he is your son, and even if
he harmed you with the most immoral act,
for you to take revenge by hurting him,
father, would not be right. So let him come.
Other men have evil sons who make them
intensely angry, but when they listen
to advice from friends, then, as if spellbound,
their mood softens and they are pacified.
Set aside the present—think of the past,
the sufferings your parents made you bear.
If you consider that, then I am sure
you'll recognize how an evil temper
can lead to catastrophic consequences.
This is a serious matter, and you
have every reason to reflect on it—
you have no eyes and can no longer see.[42]
Do what we ask. For it is not proper
that those pleading on behalf of justice
should have to persist with their entreaties,
nor is it appropriate that someone
who has been treated kindly does not know
how to show such kindness in return.

OEDIPUS

My child,
what you desire is difficult for me.
However, your speech has won me over.
We will do as you wish. But still, my friend,
if that man does come here, I only pray
that no one will end up controlling me.

Θησευσ

ἅπαξ τὰ τοιαῦτ', οὐχὶ δὶς χρῄζω κλύειν,
ὦ πρέσβυ. κομπεῖν δ' οὐχὶ βούλομαι· σὺ δ' ὢν
σῶς ἴσθ', ἐάν περ κἀμέ τις σῴζῃ θεῶν.

Χοροσ

ὅστις τοῦ πλέονος μέρους χρῄζει τοῦ μετρίου παρεὶς
ζώειν, σκαιοσύναν φυλάσσων ἐν ἐμοὶ κατάδηλος ἔσται.
ἐπεὶ πολλὰ μὲν αἱ μακραὶ ἁμέραι κατέθεντο δὴ
λύπας ἐγγυτέρω, τὰ τέρποντα δ' οὐκ ἂν ἴδοις ὅπου,
ὅταν τις ἐς πλέον πέσῃ
τοῦ δέοντος· ὁ δ' ἐπίκουρος ἰσοτέλεστος,
Ἄϊδος ὅτε μοῖρ' ἀνυμέναιος
ἄλυρος ἄχορος ἀναπέφηνε,
θάνατος ἐς τελευτάν.

μὴ φῦναι τὸν ἅπαντα νικᾷ λόγον· τὸ δ', ἐπεὶ φανῇ,
βῆναι κεῖθεν ὅθεν περ ἥκει, πολὺ δεύτερον, ὡς τάχιστα.
ὡς εὖτ' ἂν τὸ νέον παρῇ κούφας ἀφροσύνας φέρον,
τίς πλαγὰ πολύμοχθος ἔξω; τίς οὐ καμάτων ἔνι;
φθόνος, στάσεις, ἔρις, μάχαι
καὶ φόνοι· τό τε κατάμεμπτον ἐπιλέλογχε
πύματον ἀκρατὲς ἀπροσόμιλον
γῆρας ἄφιλον, ἵνα πρόπαντα
κακὰ κακῶν ξυνοικεῖ.

ἐν ᾧ τλάμων ὅδ', οὐκ ἐγὼ μόνος,
πάντοθεν βόρειος ὥς τις
ἀκτὰ κυματοπλὴξ χειμερία κλονεῖται,
ὣς καὶ τόνδε κατ' ἄκρας
δειναὶ κυματοαγεῖς
ἆται κλονέουσιν ἀεὶ ξυνοῦσαι,
αἱ μὲν ἀπ' ἀελίου δυσμᾶν,
αἱ δ' ἀνατέλλοντος·
αἱ δ' ἀνὰ μέσσαν ἀκτῖν',
αἱ δ' ἐννυχιᾶν ἀπὸ Ῥιπᾶν.

THESEUS

I do not need to hear you say that twice.
Once is enough. I do not wish to boast,
old man, but you should surely understand
you are quite safe, if gods keep me alive.

[THESEUS and his ATTENDANTS leave]

CHORUS

A man desperate for many years of life,
not content to live a moderate span,
is, in my judgment, obviously a fool.
For many feelings stored by lengthy years
evoke more pain than joy, and when we live
beyond those years that are appropriate,
then our delights are nowhere to be found.
The same Deliverer visits all of us,
and when our fate from Hades comes at last,
there is no music, dance, or wedding song—
no—only the finality of Death.

The finest of all possibilities
is never to be born, but if a man
sees the light of day, the next best thing by far
is to return as quickly as he can,
to go back to the place from which he came.
For once the careless follies of his youth
have passed, what harsh affliction is he spared,
what suffering does he not undergo?
Envy and quarrels, murder, strife and war,
until at last he reaches his old age,
rejected and alone, unloved and weak,
a state where every form of sadness dwells.

That is where I live, but not alone,
for suffering Oedipus is there as well—
like some north-facing cliff beside the sea
lashed on every side by winter blasts,
beaten constantly by breaking waves
of violent disaster, storms which come
from western regions of the setting sun,
or eastern countries where it rises,
or southern realms of noontime heat,
or northern mountains, dark as night.

ΑΝΤΙΓΟΝΗ

καὶ μὴν ὅδ' ἡμῖν, ὡς ἔοικεν, ὁ ξένος
ἀνδρῶν γε μοῦνος, ὦ πάτερ, δι' ὄμματος
ἀστακτὶ λείβων δάκρυον ὧδ' ὁδοιπορεῖ.

ΟΙΔΙΠΟΥΣ

τίς οὗτος;

ΑΝΤΙΓΟΝΗ

ὅνπερ καὶ πάλαι κατείχομεν
γνώμῃ, πάρεστι δεῦρο Πολυνείκης ὅδε.

ΠΟΛΥΝΕΙΚΗΣ

οἴμοι, τί δράσω; πότερα τἀμαυτοῦ κακὰ
πρόσθεν δακρύσω, παῖδες, ἢ τὰ τοῦδ' ὁρῶν
πατρὸς γέροντος; ὃς ξένης ἐπὶ χθονὸς
σὺν σφῷν ἐφηύρηκ' ἐνθάδ' ἐκβεβλημένον
ἐσθῆτι σὺν τοιᾷδε, τῆς ὁ δυσφιλὴς
γέρων γέροντι συγκατῴκηκεν πίνος
πλευρὰν μαραίνων, κρατὶ δ' ὀμματοστερεῖ
κόμη δι' αὔρας ἀκτένιστος ᾄσσεται·
ἀδελφὰ δ', ὡς ἔοικε, τούτοισιν φορεῖ
τὰ τῆς ταλαίνης νηδύος θρεπτήρια.
ἁγὼ πανώλης ὄψ' ἄγαν ἐκμανθάνω·
καὶ μαρτυρῶ κάκιστος ἀνθρώπων τροφαῖς
ταῖς σαῖσιν ἥκειν· τἀμὰ μὴ 'ξ ἄλλων πύθῃ.
ἀλλ' ἔστι γὰρ καὶ Ζηνὶ σύνθακος θρόνων
Αἰδὼς ἐπ' ἔργοις πᾶσι, καὶ πρὸς σοί, πάτερ,
παρασταθήτω· τῶν γὰρ ἡμαρτημένων
ἄκη μὲν ἔστι, προσφορὰ δ' οὐκ ἔστ' ἔτι.
τί σιγᾷς;
φώνησον, ὦ πάτερ, τι· μή μ' ἀποστραφῇς.
οὐδ' ἀνταμείβει μ' οὐδέν, ἀλλ' ἀτιμάσας
πέμψεις ἄναυδος, οὐδ' ἃ μηνίεις φράσας;

ANTIGONE

Look there! It appears as if the stranger
is coming here alone, without an escort.
Father, he has tears streaming from his eyes.

OEDIPUS

Who is he?

ANTIGONE

The one we talked about just now—
it's Polyneices. He's coming closer!

[Enter POLYNEICES. He greets ANTIGONE and ISMENE first.]

POLYNEICES

Alas, my sisters, how should I begin?
Should I lament my own misfortunes first
or my father's troubles? I see him here,
an old man, and I find him with you
cast out in a foreign land, an exile,
dressed in such disgusting clothes—so filthy
the grime from years ago is now engrained
in his old flesh, putrefying his skin.
Above those empty sockets in his face
his wild dishevelled hair blows in the wind,
and I suppose the food he has with him
is just the same, scraps for his poor belly.
I am a wretch to learn of this too late!

[POLYNEICES turns his attention to OEDIPUS.]

I admit that in the care I've shown for you
I've proved myself the very worst of men—
and I'm the one confessing this to you!
But since in all he does Zeus shares his throne
with divine Compassion, let that goddess
inspire you, father. For the wrongs I did
can be made good—I cannot make them worse.
Why are you silent? Say something, father.
Do not turn aside! Will you not answer me?
Will you dishonour me—send me away
without uttering a word or telling me
why you are so angry?

ὦ σπέρματ᾽ ἀνδρὸς τοῦδ᾽, ἐμαὶ δ᾽ ὁμαίμονες,
πειράσατ᾽ ἀλλ᾽ ὑμεῖς γε κινῆσαι πατρὸς
τὸ δυσπρόσοιστον κἀπροσήγορον στόμα,
ὡς μή μ᾽ ἄτιμον, τοῦ θεοῦ γε προστάτην,
οὕτως ἀφῇ με μηδὲν ἀντειπὼν ἔπος.

ΑΝΤΙΓΟΝΗ

λέγ᾽, ὦ ταλαίπωρ᾽, αὐτὸς ὧν χρείᾳ πάρει·
τὰ πολλὰ γάρ τοι ῥήματ᾽ ἢ τέρψαντά τι,
ἢ δυσχεράναντ᾽ ἢ κατοικτίσαντά πως,
παρέσχε φωνὴν τοῖς ἀφωνήτοις τινά.

ΠΟΛΥΝΕΙΚΗΣ

ἀλλ᾽ ἐξερῶ· καλῶς γὰρ ἐξηγεῖ σύ μοι·
πρῶτον μὲν αὐτὸν τὸν θεὸν ποιούμενος
ἀρωγόν, ἔνθεν μ᾽ ὧδ᾽ ἀνέστησεν μολεῖν
ὁ τῆσδε τῆς γῆς κοίρανος, διδοὺς ἐμοὶ
λέξαι τ᾽ ἀκοῦσαί τ᾽ ἀσφαλεῖ σὺν ἐξόδῳ.
καὶ ταῦτ᾽ ἀφ᾽ ὑμῶν, ὦ ξένοι, βουλήσομαι
καὶ ταῖνδ᾽ ἀδελφαῖν καὶ πατρὸς κυρεῖν ἐμοί.
ἃ δ᾽ ἦλθον, ἤδη σοι θέλω λέξαι, πάτερ.
γῆς ἐκ πατρῴας ἐξελήλαμαι φυγάς,
τοῖς σοῖς πανάρχοις οὕνεκ᾽ ἐνθακεῖν θρόνοις
γονῇ πεφυκὼς ἠξίουν γεραίτερος.
ἀνθ᾽ ὧν μ᾽ Ἐτεοκλῆς, ὢν φύσει νεώτερος,
γῆς ἐξέωσεν, οὔτε νικήσας λόγῳ
οὔτ᾽ εἰς ἔλεγχον χειρὸς οὐδ᾽ ἔργου μολών,
πόλιν δὲ πείσας. ὧν ἐγὼ μάλιστα μὲν
τὴν σὴν ἐρινὺν αἰτίαν εἶναι λέγω.
ἔπειτα κἀπὸ μάντεων ταύτῃ κλύω.
ἐπεὶ γὰρ ἦλθον Ἄργος ἐς τὸ Δωρικόν,
λαβὼν Ἄδραστον πενθερόν, ξυνωμότας
ἔστησ᾽ ἐμαυτῷ γῆς ὅσοιπερ Ἀπίας
πρῶτοι καλοῦνται καὶ τετίμηνται δόρει,

[OEDIPUS refuses to acknowledge POLYNEICES]

Come, my sisters,
you are this man's daughters. You, above all,
should try to ease that stubborn tongue Of his
which makes him so difficult to talk to.
Otherwise he will never speak to me
and will dismiss me in disgrace from here,
where I stand a suppliant to the gods.

ANTIGONE

You poor unfortunate, tell him yourself
the reason you came here. A moving speech
may well awaken pleasure, rage, or pity
and rouse a silent listener to speak.

POLYNEICES

You have advised me well. I will speak out.
And to begin with, I appeal for help
to lord Poseidon, for at his altar
the king of Athens told me to stand up
and come here, giving me assurances
I could listen and speak and leave unharmed.
I trust these promises will be observed,
strangers, by you, by both my sisters here,
and by my father, too. And now, father,
I want to tell you the reason I am here.
I have been driven from my native land
into exile because, as your elder son,
I thought the right to sit upon your throne
and wield your royal power belonged to me.
But then Eteocles, my younger brother,
forced me out of Thebes, not by prevailing
with legal arguments or trial by combat,
but by persuading Thebes to back his side.
The most important cause of this, in my view,
is that old curse placed on your family,
an opinion I have heard from prophets, too.
And so I went to Dorian Argos,
made king Adrastus my father-in-law,
and bound to me as sworn companions
all the most celebrated warriors
in Apian lands, so that with these allies

ὅπως τὸν ἑπτάλογχον ἐς Θήβας στόλον
ξὺν τοῖσδ᾽ ἀγείρας ἢ θάνοιμι πανδίκως
ἢ τοὺς τάδ᾽ ἐκπράξαντας ἐκβάλοιμι γῆς.
εἶεν· τί δῆτα νῦν ἀφιγμένος κυρῶ;
σοὶ προστροπαίους, ὦ πάτερ, λιτὰς ἔχων
αὐτός τ᾽ ἐμαυτοῦ ξυμμάχων τε τῶν ἐμῶν,
οἳ νῦν σὺν ἑπτὰ τάξεσιν σὺν ἑπτά τε
λόγχαις τὸ Θήβης πέδιον ἀμφεστᾶσι πᾶν·
οἷος δορυσσοῦς Ἀμφιάρεως, τὰ πρῶτα μὲν
δόρει κρατύνων, πρῶτα δ᾽ οἰωνῶν ὁδοῖς·
ὁ δεύτερος δ᾽ Αἰτωλὸς Οἰνέως τόκος
Τυδεύς. τρίτος δ᾽ Ἐτέοκλος, Ἀργεῖος γεγώς·
τέταρτον Ἱππομέδοντ᾽ ἀπέστειλεν πατὴρ
Ταλαός· ὁ πέμπτος δ᾽ εὔχεται κατασκαφῇ
Καπανεὺς τὸ Θήβης ἄστυ δῃώσειν πυρί·
ἕκτος δὲ Παρθενοπαῖος Ἀρκὰς ὄρνυται,
ἐπώνυμος τῆς πρόσθεν ἀδμήτης χρόνῳ
μητρὸς λοχευθείς, πιστὸς Ἀταλάντης γόνος·
ἐγὼ δὲ σός, κεἰ μὴ σός, ἀλλὰ τοῦ κακοῦ
πότμου φυτευθείς, σός γέ τοι καλούμενος,
ἄγω τὸν Ἄργους ἄφοβον ἐς Θήβας στρατόν.
οἵ σ᾽ ἀντὶ παίδων τῶνδε καὶ ψυχῆς, πάτερ,
ἱκετεύομεν ξύμπαντες ἐξαιτούμενοι
μῆνιν βαρεῖαν εἰκαθεῖν ὁρμωμένῳ
τῷδ᾽ ἀνδρὶ τοὐμοῦ πρὸς κασιγνήτου τίσιν,
ὅς μ᾽ ἐξέωσε κἀπεσύλησεν πάτρας.
εἰ γάρ τι πιστόν ἐστιν ἐκ χρηστηρίων,
οἷς ἂν σὺ προσθῇ, τοῖσδ᾽ ἔφασκ᾽ εἶναι κράτος.
πρὸς νῦν σε κρηνῶν καὶ θεῶν ὁμογνίων
αἰτῶ πιθέσθαι καὶ παρεικαθεῖν, ἐπεὶ
πτωχοὶ μὲν ἡμεῖς καὶ ξένοι, ξένος δὲ σύ.

I might levy an armed force of spearmen
in seven companies to march on Thebes
and die in a just cause or else drive out
the people who had treated me this way.[43]
What then do I now seek by coming here?
Father, I have come to you in person
pleading for your help—with prayers from me
and from my comrades, those seven spearmen,
who with their seven armies now surround
the entire Theban plain. Of those leaders,
one is spear-hurling Amphiaraus,
an expert warrior and preeminent
in reading omens in the flights of birds.
The second chieftain there is Tydeus,
from Aetolia, son of Oeneus.
The third is Argive-born Eteoclus;
the fourth is Hippomedon, sent to Thebes
by Talaos, his father. The fifth of them,
Capaneus, boasts he will burn Thebes
and utterly obliterate the city.
The sixth, Arcadian Parthenopaeus,
is eager for the fight. He gets his name
from Atalanta, who was his mother.
She remained a virgin for many years
before she married and gave birth to him.[44]
I am the seventh of them, your own son,
or if not yours, a child of evil fate,
although I may be yours in name.[45] I've brought
to Thebes a valiant force of Argives.
Each and every one of us implores you,
as you love your daughters and your life,
pleading with you, father, to put aside
that oppressive rage you feel against me,
as I set out to pay my brother back.
He forced me into exile and robbed me
of my native land. For if we can trust
in prophecy, then those allied with you,
so say the oracles, will win the day.
So by our fountains and our family gods,
I'm begging you to listen and relent.
For I am a stranger and a beggar
on foreign soil, and so are you, as well.

ἄλλους δὲ θωπεύοντες οἰκοῦμεν σύ τε
κἀγώ, τὸν αὐτὸν δαίμον᾽ ἐξειληχότες.
ὁ δ᾽ ἐν δόμοις τύραννος, ὢ τάλας ἐγώ,
κοινῇ καθ᾽ ἡμῶν ἐγγελῶν ἁβρύνεται·
ὅν, εἰ σὺ τἠμῇ ξυμπαραστήσει φρενί,
βραχεῖ σὺν ὄγκῳ καὶ χρόνῳ διασκεδῶ.
ὥστ᾽ ἐν δόμοισι τοῖσι σοῖς στήσω σ᾽ ἄγων.
στήσω δ᾽ ἐμαυτόν, κεῖνον ἐκβαλὼν βίᾳ.
καὶ ταῦτα σοῦ μὲν ξυνθέλοντος ἔστι μοι
κομπεῖν, ἄνευ σοῦ δ᾽ οὐδὲ σωθῆναι σθένω.

Χορος

τὸν ἄνδρα τοῦ πέμψαντος οὕνεκ᾽, Οἰδίπους
εἰπὼν ὁποῖα ξύμφορ᾽ ἔκπεμψαι πάλιν.

Οιδιπους

ἀλλ᾽ εἰ μέν, ἄνδρες, τῆσδε δημοῦχοι χθονός
μὴ ᾽τύγχαν᾽ αὐτὸν δεῦρο προσπέμψας ἐμοὶ
Θησεύς, δικαιῶν ὥστ᾽ ἐμοῦ κλύειν λόγους,
οὔ τἄν ποτ᾽ ὀμφῆς τῆς ἐμῆς ἐπῄσθετο·
νῦν δ᾽ ἀξιωθεὶς εἶσι κἀκούσας γ᾽ ἐμοῦ
τοιαῦθ᾽ ἃ τὸν τοῦδ᾽ οὔ ποτ᾽ εὐφρανεῖ βίον·
ὅς γ᾽, ὦ κάκιστε, σκῆπτρα καὶ θρόνους ἔχων,
ἃ νῦν ὁ σὸς ξύναιμος ἐν Θήβαις ἔχει,
τὸν αὐτὸς αὑτοῦ πατέρα τόνδ᾽ ἀπήλασας
κἄθηκας ἄπολιν καὶ στολὰς ταύτας φορεῖν,
ἃς νῦν δακρύεις εἰσορῶν, ὅτ᾽ ἐν πόνῳ
ταὐτῷ βεβηκὼς τυγχάνεις κακῶν ἐμοί.
οὐ κλαυστὰ δ᾽ ἐστίν, ἀλλ᾽ ἐμοὶ μὲν οἰστέα
τάδ᾽, ἕωσπερ ἂν ζῶ, σοῦ φονέως μεμνημένος·
σὺ γάρ με μόχθῳ τῷδ᾽ ἔθηκας ἔντροφον,

You and I both share a similar fate—
we get a place to live by flattery,
paying court to others, while my brother,
unhappily for me, lives in the palace,
an arrogant tyrant mocking both of us.
If you become our ally in this fight,
I'll scatter his armed forces to the winds—
that won't be difficult or take much time—
and then I'll bring you back and set you up
in your own home and me in mine and drive
Eteocles away by force. All this
I promise to achieve with your support.
Without you, I shall not return alive.

CHORUS
For the sake of the king who sent him here,
Oedipus, make a suitable response
before you send him on his way.

OEDIPUS *[to the CHORUS]*
You men,
guardians of this land, if Theseus
were not the one who sent this man to me,
thinking it right that I should speak to him,
then he would never hear me say a word.
But since you all insist he ought to have
an audience with me before he leaves,
let him hear what I have to say—my words
will never bring his life the slightest joy.

[OEDIPUS turns his attention to POLYNEICES]

You there, you most despicable of men,
when you were on the throne and held the sceptre,
the power your brother now wields in Thebes,
you hounded me, your father, from the land,
pushed me into exile, and made me wear
these garments which, when you look at them now,
bring tears into your eyes, because you find
your life is just as miserable as mine![46]
For me there is no point in shedding tears—
while I am still alive, I must endure it,
remembering that you're my murderer.
You forced me to live in this wretched state!

σύ μ᾿ ἐξέωσας, ἐκ σέθεν δ᾿ ἀλώμενος
ἄλλους ἐπαιτῶ τὸν καθ᾿ ἡμέραν βίον.
εἰ δ᾿ ἐξέφυσα τάσδε μὴ ᾿μαυτῷ τροφοὺς
τὰς παῖδας, ἦ τἂν οὐκ ἂν ἦ, τὸ σὸν μέρος·
νῦν δ᾿ αἵδε μ᾿ ἐκσῴζουσιν, αἵδ᾿ ἐμαὶ τροφοί,
αἵδ᾿ ἄνδρες, οὐ γυναῖκες, εἰς τὸ συμπονεῖν·
ὑμεῖς δ᾿ ἀπ᾿ ἄλλου κοὐκ ἐμοῦ πεφύκατον.
τοιγάρ σ᾿ ὁ δαίμων εἰσορᾷ μὲν οὔ τί πω
ὡς αὐτίκ᾿, εἴπερ οἵδε κινοῦνται λόχοι
πρὸς ἄστυ Θήβης. οὐ γὰρ ἔσθ᾿ ὅπως πόλιν
κείνην ἐρείψεις, ἀλλὰ πρόσθεν αἵματι
πεσεῖ μιανθεὶς χὠ σύναιμος ἐξ ἴσου.
τοιάσδ᾿ ἀρὰς σφῷν πρόσθε τ᾿ ἐξανῆκ᾿ ἐγὼ
νῦν τ᾿ ἀνακαλοῦμαι ξυμμάχους ἐλθεῖν ἐμοί,
ἵν᾿ ἀξιῶτον τοὺς φυτεύσαντας σέβειν
καὶ μὴ ᾿ξατιμάζητον, εἰ τυφλοῦ πατρὸς
τοιώδ᾿ ἐφύτην· αἵδε γὰρ τάδ᾿ οὐκ ἔδρων.
τοιγὰρ τὸ σὸν θάκημα καὶ τοὺς σοὺς θρόνους
κρατοῦσιν, εἴπερ ἐστὶν ἡ παλαίφατος
Δίκη ξύνεδρος Ζηνὸς ἀρχαίοις νόμοις.
σὺ δ᾿ ἔρρ᾿ ἀπόπτυστός τε κἀπάτωρ ἐμοῦ,
κακῶν κάκιστε, τάσδε συλλαβὼν ἀράς,
ἅς σοι καλοῦμαι, μήτε γῆς ἐμφυλίου
δόρει κρατῆσαι μήτε νοστῆσαί ποτε
τὸ κοῖλον Ἄργος, ἀλλὰ συγγενεῖ χερὶ
θανεῖν κτανεῖν θ᾿ ὑφ᾿ οὗπερ ἐξελήλασαι.
τοιαῦτ᾿ ἀρῶμαι καὶ καλῶ τὸ Ταρτάρου
στυγνὸν πατρῷον ἔρεβος, ὥς σ᾿ ἀποικίσῃ,
καλῶ δὲ τάσδε δαίμονας, καλῶ δ᾿ Ἄρη
τὸν σφῷν τὸ δεινὸν μῖσος ἐμβεβληκότα.

You two banished me, and because of you,
I am a vagrant, begging every day
for bread from strangers. If I had not fathered
these two daughters, who serve as my support,
I would have died for lack of help from you.
But now these girls are looking after me—
they provide for me and share my suffering.
They are like men, not women. But you two,
you are both bastards, born from someone else,
no sons of mine! And so the eye of god
is watching you—but not as it will soon,
if your armies mean to march on Thebes.
For you will never overwhelm that city.
Before that happens, you and your brother
will fall, polluted by each other's blood.
And now I summon those very curses
I called down earlier against you both.
I cry to them to come to my assistance,
so that the two of you will understand
those who bore you are worthy of respect.[47]
It is not right to treat them with contempt,
because a father who had sons like you
has lost his eyes. These girls did not do that.
And so if Justice established long ago
and sanctioned by our ancient laws still sits
alongside Zeus, these curses I call down
will overpower your suppliant prayers
and all claims to the throne.[48] Get out of here!
I spit you out! You are no son of mine!
You most contemptible of evil men!
Take with you these prayers I make on your behalf—
may your armies never overwhelm that land
where you were born, may you never return
to the land of Argos, but rather die
at the hand of the one of your own kinsmen,
and kill the man who drove you out of Thebes!
That is what I pray for. And I call on
the dreadful paternal dark of Tartarus
to deliver you to your new dwelling place.[49]
I invoke the spirits here, the Furies,
and summon Ares, god of war, who set
such lethal hatred in the two of you!

καὶ ταῦτ᾽ ἀκούσας στεῖχε, κἀξάγγελλ᾽ ἰὼν
καὶ πᾶσι Καδμείοισι τοῖς σαυτοῦ θ᾽ ἅμα
πιστοῖσι συμμάχοισιν, οὕνεκ᾽ Οἰδίπους
τοιαῦτ᾽ ἔνειμε παισὶ τοῖς αὑτοῦ γέρα.

Χορος

Πολύνεικες, οὔτε ταῖς παρελθούσαις ὁδοῖς
ξυνήδομαί σοι, νῦν τ᾽ ἴθ᾽ ὡς τάχος πάλιν.

Πολυνεικης

οἴμοι κελεύθου τῆς τ᾽ ἐμῆς δυσπραξίας,
οἴμοι δ᾽ ἑταίρων· οἷον ἆρ᾽ ὁδοῦ τέλος
Ἄργους ἀφωρμήθημεν, ὢ τάλας ἐγώ,
τοιοῦτον οἷον οὐδὲ φωνῆσαί τινι
ἔξεσθ᾽ ἑταίρων, οὐδ᾽ ἀποστρέψαι πάλιν,
ἀλλ᾽ ὄντ᾽ ἄναυδον τῇδε συγκῦρσαι τύχῃ.
ὦ τοῦδ᾽ ὅμαιμοι παῖδες, ἀλλ᾽ ὑμεῖς, ἐπεὶ
τὰ σκληρὰ πατρὸς κλύετε ταῦτ᾽ ἀρωμένου,
μή τοί με πρὸς θεῶν σφώ γ᾽, ἐὰν αἱ τοῦδ᾽ ἀραὶ
πατρὸς τελῶνται καί τις ὑμὶν ἐς δόμους
νόστος γένηται, μή μ᾽ ἀτιμάσητέ γε,
ἀλλ᾽ ἐν τάφοισι θέσθε κἀν κτερίσμασιν.
καὶ σφῷν ὁ νῦν ἔπαινος, ὃν κομίζετον
τοῦδ᾽, ἀνδρὸς οἷς πονεῖτον, οὐκ ἐλάσσονα
ἔτ᾽ ἄλλον οἴσει τῆς ἐμῆς ὑπουργίας.

Αντιγονη

Πολύνεικες, ἱκετεύω σε πεισθῆναί τί μοι.

Πολυνεικης

ὦ φιλτάτη, τὸ ποῖον, Ἀντιγόνη; λέγε.

Αντιγονη

στρέψαι στράτευμ᾽ ἐς Ἄργος ὡς τάχιστά γε,
καὶ μὴ σέ τ᾽ αὐτὸν καὶ πόλιν διεργάσῃ.

Πολυνεικης

ἀλλ᾽ οὐχ οἷόν τε. πῶς γὰρ αὖθις ἂν πάλιν
στράτευμ᾽ ἄγοιμι ταὐτόν. εἰσάπαξ τρέσας;

You have heard what I have spoken. Now leave.
Proclaim to all the citizens of Thebes
and to your loyal confederates, as well,
that Oedipus has handed out these gifts
as royal bequests to his two sons.

CHORUS

Polyneices,
the journey you have made brings me no joy—
and now you must return without delay.

POLYNEICES

So much for my trip here—it's a disaster.
Alas for my companions! This is the end
of the road we marched when we left Argos—
unhappily for me! I cannot speak of this
to any of my friends or turn them back.
I must stay silent and confront my fate.
But you, my sisters, daughters of this man,
you have heard our father's brutal curses.
If what he is praying for is fulfilled
and you get back to Thebes, then I beg you,
by all the gods, do not leave my body
to be dishonored. Set me in a tomb,
and have me buried with full funeral rites.
If you do that, the praises you both earn
from this man for the help you two provide
will be increased by no less generous praise
you will receive for looking after me.

ANTIGONE

Polyneices, listen to me, I beg you!

POLYNEICES

Dearest Antigone, what is it? Speak out.

ANTIGONE

Turn your forces back—and do it quickly.
Return to Argos. Do not ravage Thebes
and destroy yourself.

POLYNEICES

That is not possible.
Once I turn back because I am afraid,
how could I ever lead that force again?

ΑΝΤΙΓΟΝΗ

τί δ' αὖθις, ὦ παῖ, δεῖ σε θυμοῦσθαι; τί σοι
πάτραν κατασκάψαντι κέρδος ἔρχεται;

ΠΟΛΥΝΕΙΚΗΣ

αἰσχρὸν τὸ φεύγειν καὶ τὸ πρεσβεύοντ' ἐμὲ
οὕτω γελᾶσθαι τοῦ κασιγνήτου πάρα.

ΑΝΤΙΓΟΝΗ

ὁρᾷς τὰ τοῦδ' οὖν ὡς ἐς ὀρθὸν ἐκφέρει
μαντεύμαθ', ὃς σφῷν θάνατον ἐξ ἀμφοῖν θροεῖ;

ΠΟΛΥΝΕΙΚΗΣ

χρῄζει γάρ· ἡμῖν δ' οὐχὶ συγχωρητέα.

ΑΝΤΙΓΟΝΗ

οἴμοι τάλαινα· τίς δὲ τολμήσει κλύων
τὰ τοῦδ' ἕπεσθαι τἀνδρός, οἷ' ἐθέσπισεν;

ΠΟΛΥΝΕΙΚΗΣ

οὐκ ἀγγελοῦμεν φλαῦρ'· ἐπεὶ στρατηλάτου
χρηστοῦ τὰ κρείσσω μηδὲ τἀνδεᾶ λέγειν.

ΑΝΤΙΓΟΝΗ

οὕτως ἄρ', ὦ παῖ, ταῦτά σοι δεδογμένα;

ΠΟΛΥΝΕΙΚΗΣ

καὶ μή μ' ἐπίσχῃς γ'· ἀλλ' ἐμοὶ μὲν ἥδ' ὁδὸς
ἔσται μέλουσα δύσποτμός τε καὶ κακὴ
πρὸς τοῦδε πατρὸς τῶν τε τοῦδ' ἐρινύων·
σφῷν δ' εὖ διδοίη Ζεύς, τάδ' εἰ θανόντι μοι
τελεῖτ', ἐπεὶ οὔ μοι ζῶντί γ' αὖθις ἕξετον.
μέθεσθε δ' ἤδη χαίρετόν τ'· οὐ γάρ μ' ἔτι
βλέποντ' ἐσόψεσθ' αὖθις.

Antigone

Again? Why, brother, would you ever again
get so angry? How do you benefit
from destroying the city of your birth?

Polyneices

It is dishonourable to live in exile
and to be made a laughing stock like this,
when I'm the elder son.

Antigone

But don't you see
you will be confirming the prophecies
our father uttered? They are predicting
you and Eteocles will kill each other.

Polyneices

That's what he wants. But I cannot give up.

Antigone

Alas, that is insufferable for me!
But who will follow you once he has heard
what has been prophesied?

Polyneices

I will not tell them
such a grim prediction. A proper leader
conveys good things and hides unwelcome news.

Antigone

Are you resolved to do this, my brother?

Polyneices

I am. Do not attempt to hold me back.
This ill-fated, catastrophic path is now
the one destined for me, thanks to my father
and his avenging Furies. But for you two,
my sisters, may Zeus provide rich favours,
if you will carry out full burial rites
for me when I am dead. There's nothing more
you can perform for me while I still live.
So let me set out on my way. Farewell.
You will not see me in this life again.

Ἀντιγονη

ὢ τάλαιν᾽ ἐγώ.

Πολυνεικης

μή τοί μ᾽ ὀδύρου.

Ἀντιγονη

καὶ τίς ἄν σ᾽ ὁρμώμενον
εἰς προὖπτον Ἅιδην οὐ καταστένοι, κάσι;

Πολυνεικης

εἰ χρή, θανοῦμαι.

Ἀντιγονη

μὴ σύ γ᾽, ἀλλ᾽ ἐμοὶ πιθοῦ.

Πολυνεικης

μὴ πεῖθ᾽ ἃ μὴ δεῖ.

Ἀντιγονη

δυστάλαινά τἄρ᾽ ἐγώ,
εἴ σου στερηθῶ.

Πολυνεικης

ταῦτα δ᾽ ἐν τῷ δαίμονι
καὶ τῇδε φῦναι χἀτέρᾳ. σφῷν δ᾽ οὖν ἐγὼ
θεοῖς ἀρῶμαι μή ποτ᾽ ἀντῆσαι κακῶν·
ἀνάξιαι γὰρ πᾶσίν ἐστε δυστυχεῖν.

Χορος

νέα τάδε νεόθεν ἦλθέ μοι
κακὰ βαρύποτμα παρ᾽ ἀλαοῦ ξένου,
εἴ τι μοῖρα μὴ κιγχάνει.
μάταν γὰρ οὐδὲν ἀξίωμα δαιμόνων ἔχω φράσαι.
ὁρᾷ ὁρᾷ ταῦτ᾽ ἀεὶ χρόνος, τρέχων μὲν ἕτερα,
τὰ δὲ παρ᾽ ἦμαρ αὖθις αὔξων ἄνω.
ἔκτυπεν αἰθήρ, ὦ Ζεῦ.

ANTIGONE
I am so wretched!

POLYNEICES
Do not feel sad for me.

ANTIGONE
Who would not feel sad for you, my brother,
when you are marching off to certain death?

POLYNEICES
If it is my fate, then I shall die.

Antigone
No!
Listen to me instead!

POLYNEICES
Do not keep pleading
for what will never happen.

ANTIGONE
If I lose you,
my life will have no joy.

POLYNEICES
Fate will decide
one way or the other. As for you both,
may gods grant you never meet disaster,
for all men know you two do not deserve
a life of suffering and misery.

[POLYNEICES leaves. There is a rumble of thunder in the distance.]

CHORUS
I sense the approach of fresh misfortune,
a new load of grief from this blind stranger,
unless Fate is now perhaps approaching
its predestined end, for I cannot say
decisions of the gods stay unfulfilled.
Time keeps watch and always sees these things—
one day it casts some down, and on the next
it raises others up once more.

[There is another peal of thunder, this time much closer than before.]

O Zeus,
your heavenly skies reverberate!

Οιδιπους

ὦ τέκνα τέκνα, πῶς ἄν, εἴ τις ἔντοπος,
τὸν πάντ᾽ ἄριστον δεῦρο Θησέα πόροι;

Αντιγονη

πάτερ, τί δ᾽ ἐστὶ τἀξίωμ᾽ ἐφ᾽ ᾧ καλεῖς;

Οιδιπους

Διὸς πτερωτὸς ἥδε μ᾽ αὐτίκ᾽ ἄξεται
βροντὴ πρὸς Ἅιδην· ἀλλὰ πέμψαθ᾽ ὡς τάχος.

Χορος

μέγας, ἴδε, μάλ᾽ ὅδ᾽ ἐρείπεται
κτύπος ἄφατος διόβολος· ἐς δ᾽ ἄκραν
δεῖμ᾽ ὑπῆλθε κρατὸς φόβαν.
ἔπτηξα θυμόν· οὐρανία γὰρ ἀστραπὴ φλέγει πάλιν.
τί μὰν ἀφήσει τέλος; δέδοικα δ᾽· οὐ γὰρ ἅλιον
ἀφορμᾷ ποτ᾽, οὐκ ἄνευ ξυμφορᾶς.
ὦ μέγας αἰθήρ, ὦ Ζεῦ.

Οιδιπους

ὦ παῖδες, ἥκει τῷδ᾽ ἐπ᾽ ἀνδρὶ θέσφατος
βίου τελευτὴ κοὐκέτ᾽ ἔστ᾽ ἀποστροφή.

Αντιγονη

πῶς οἶσθα; τῷ δὲ τοῦτο συμβαλὼν ἔχεις;

Οιδιπους

καλῶς κάτοιδ᾽· ἀλλ᾽ ὡς τάχιστά μοι μολὼν
ἄνακτα χώρας τῆσδέ τις πορευσάτω.

Χορος

ἔα ἔα, ἰδοὺ μάλ᾽ αὖθις ἀμφίσταται διαπρύσιος ὄτοβος.

OEDIPUS

My children, if there is anyone here,
tell him to summon Theseus back,
that finest of all men.

ANTIGONE

Why, father?
Why do you want us to send for Theseus?

OEDIPUS

Zeus' winged thunder will soon lead me
on to Hades. Send someone now—and quickly!

[Thunder peals again, sounding very close, and lightning flashes.]

CHORUS

Listen! The crash of an immense thunderbolt
hurled down by Zeus—my scalp bristles,
overwhelmed with fear, my heart recoils!

Lightning blazes once more through the sky!
What final purposes are being revealed?

I am afraid. Such fire from Zeus
never flashes down in vain, not without
some great calamity.

[Another peal of thunder breaks above them.]

O mighty heavens! O Zeus!

OEDIPUS

My children, for me the destined end of life
is drawing near. There is no turning back.

Antigone

How do you know? What signs have you received?

OEDIPUS

I sense it clearly. Get someone to go
and fetch the king as quickly as he can.

[More peals of thunder and flashes of lightning.]

CHORUS

Listen! Listen to that! The piercing noise
is all around us once again!

ἵλαος, ὦ δαίμων, ἵλαος εἴ τι γᾷ
ματέρι τυγχάνεις ἀφεγγὲς φέρων.
ἐναισίου δὲ σοῦ τύχοιμι, μηδ᾽ ἄλαστον ἄνδρ᾽ ἰδὼν
ἀκερδῆ χάριν μετάσχοιμί πως. Ζεῦ ἄνα σοὶ φωνῶ.

Οιδιπουσ

ἆρ᾽ ἐγγὺς ἁνήρ; ἆρ᾽ ἔτ᾽ ἐμψύχου, τέκνα,
κιχήσεταί μου καὶ κατορθοῦντος φρένα;

Αντιγονη

τί δ᾽ ἂν θέλοις τὸ πιστὸν ἐμφῦναι φρενί;

Οιδιπουσ

ἀνθ᾽ ὧν ἔπασχον εὖ, τελεσφόρον χάριν
δοῦναί σφιν, ἥνπερ τυγχάνων ὑπεσχόμην.

Χοροσ

ἰὼ ἰὼ παῖ, βᾶθι βᾶθ᾽, εἴτ᾽ ἄκρα,
περὶ γύαλ᾽ ἐναλίῳ Ποσειδωνίῳ θεῷ, τυγχάνεις
βούθυτον ἑστίαν ἁγίζων, ἱκοῦ.
ὁ γὰρ ξένος σε καὶ πόλισμα καὶ φίλους ἐπαξιοῖ
δικαίαν χάριν παρασχεῖν παθών.
[σπεῦσον] ἄϊσσ᾽, ὦναξ.

Θησευσ

τίς αὖ παρ᾽ ὑμῶν κοινὸς ἠχεῖται κτύπος,
σαφὴς μὲν ἀστῶν, ἐμφανὴς δὲ τοῦ ξένου;

O god,
be gracious to us—show us your mercy,
if you are bringing some catastrophe
to Athens, our maternal home.

May I find you
generous to us—if I have looked upon
a man polluted by his acts, do not,
I beg you, somehow let me share his curse
or favours that bring no benefit to me![50]
O Zeus on high, I cry out to you!

OEDIPUS
My children, is lord Theseus nearby?
When he gets here will I still be alive
with my mind intact?

ANTIGONE
What trustworthy pledge
do you wish to plant within his heart?

OEDIPUS
In return for the goodwill I received,
I will do him a favour by fulfilling
everything I promised earlier.[51]

CHORUS
Come, my son, come here to us!
If you by chance are at the altar
in the deepest corner of the grove
offering an ox to god Poseidon,
lord of the sea, then come to us.
This stranger thinks it only just
that you, your city, and your friends
receive a favour for those benefits
you have so graciously conferred on him.
My lord, make haste! Come quickly!

[THESEUS enters.]

THESEUS
What is this noise? Why are you once again
all making such a din—it's clearly coming
from you citizens and from the stranger, too.

μή τις Διὸς κεραυνὸς ἤ τις ὀμβρία
χάλαζ' ἐπιρράξασα; πάντα γὰρ θεοῦ
τοιαῦτα χειμάζοντος εἰκάσαι πάρα.

ΟΙΔΙΠΟΥΣ

ἄναξ, ποθοῦντι προυφάνης, καί σοι θεῶν
τύχην τις ἐσθλὴν τῆσδ' ἔθηκε τῆς ὁδοῦ.

ΘΗΣΕΥΣ

τί δ' ἐστίν, ὦ παῖ Λαΐου, νέορτον αὖ;

ΟΙΔΙΠΟΥΣ

ῥοπὴ βίου μοι· καί σ' ἅπερ ξυνῄνεσα
θέλω πόλιν τε τήνδε μὴ ψεύσας θανεῖν.

ΘΗΣΕΥΣ

τῷ δ' ἐκπέπεισαι τοῦ μόρου τεκμηρίῳ;

ΟΙΔΙΠΟΥΣ

αὐτοὶ θεοὶ κήρυκες ἀγγέλλουσί μοι,
ψεύδοντες οὐδὲν σῆμα τῶν προκειμένων.

ΘΗΣΕΥΣ

πῶς εἶπας, ὦ γεραιέ, δηλοῦσθαι τάδε;

ΟΙΔΙΠΟΥΣ

αἱ πολλὰ βρονταὶ διατελεῖς τὰ πολλά τε
στράψαντα χειρὸς τῆς ἀνικήτου βέλη.

ΘΗΣΕΥΣ

πείθεις με· πολλὰ γάρ σε θεσπίζονθ' ὁρῶ
κοὐ ψευδόφημα· χὤ τι χρὴ ποιεῖν λέγε.

ΟΙΔΙΠΟΥΣ

ἐγὼ διδάξω, τέκνον Αἰγέως, ἅ σοι
γήρως ἄλυπα τῇδε κείσεται πόλει.
χῶρον μὲν αὐτὸς αὐτίκ' ἐξηγήσομαι,
ἄθικτος ἡγητῆρος, οὗ με χρὴ θανεῖν.

Were you frightened by a thunderbolt from Zeus
or driving showers of hail? When a god
unleashes a ferocious storm like this,
it can presage all sorts of things to come.

OEDIPUS

My lord, I have been hoping you were here—
some god has seen to it that you arrive
at a propitious time.

THESEUS

Son of Laius,
What is going on? Is it something new?

OEDIPUS

For me life moves beyond its tipping point.
I do not wish to die without confirming
the promises I made to you and Athens.

THESEUS

What omens tell you that your death is near?

OEDIPUS

The messengers who announced the news to me
are the gods themselves. They have not proven false,
for they have shown me the appointed signs.

THESEUS

What are these fatal signs, old man? Tell me.

OEDIPUS

All those frequent rolling peals of thunder
and many lightning flashes hurtling down
from an invincible hand.

THESEUS

You have convinced me.
From your many prophecies I have learned
you do not lie. Tell me what I must do.

OEDIPUS

Son of Aegeus, I will set out for you
the glories that lie in store for Athens
and that never will diminish with old age.
In a moment I myself will lead the way
to the place where I must die. I will need

τοῦτον δὲ φράζε μή ποτ᾽ ἀνθρώπων τινί,
μήθ᾽ οὗ κέκευθε μήτ᾽ ἐν οἷς κεῖται τόποις·
ὥς σοι πρὸ πολλῶν ἀσπίδων ἀλκὴν ὅδε
δορός τ᾽ ἐπακτοῦ γειτονῶν ἀεὶ τιθῇ.
ἃ δ᾽ ἐξάγιστα μηδὲ κινεῖται λόγῳ,
αὐτὸς μαθήσει, κεῖσ᾽ ὅταν μόλῃς μόνος·
ὡς οὔτ᾽ ἂν ἀστῶν τῶνδ᾽ ἂν ἐξείποιμί τῳ
οὔτ᾽ ἂν τέκνοισι τοῖς ἐμοῖς, στέργων ὅμως.
ἀλλ᾽ αὐτὸς αἰεὶ σῷζε, χὤταν εἰς τέλος
τοῦ ζῆν ἀφικνῇ, τῷ προφερτάτῳ μόνῳ
σήμαιν᾽, ὁ δ᾽ αἰεὶ τὠπιόντι δεικνύτω.
χοὔτως ἀδῇον τήνδ᾽ ἐνοικήσεις πόλιν
σπαρτῶν ἀπ᾽ ἀνδρῶν· αἱ δὲ μυρίαι πόλεις,
κἂν εὖ τις οἰκῇ, ῥᾳδίως καθύβρισαν.
θεοὶ γὰρ εὖ μέν, ὀψὲ δ᾽ εἰσορῶσ᾽, ὅταν
τὰ θεῖ᾽ ἀφείς τις εἰς τὸ μαίνεσθαι τραπῇ·
ὃ μὴ σύ, τέκνον Αἰγέως, βούλου παθεῖν.
τὰ μὲν τοιαῦτ᾽ οὖν εἰδότ᾽ ἐκδιδάσκομεν.
χῶρον δ᾽, ἐπείγει γάρ με τοὐκ θεοῦ παρόν,
στείχωμεν ἤδη μηδ᾽ ἔτ᾽ ἐντρεπώμεθα.
ὦ παῖδες, ὧδ᾽ ἕπεσθ᾽· ἐγὼ γὰρ ἡγεμὼν
σφῷν αὖ πέφασμαι καινός, ὥσπερ σφὼ πατρί.
χωρεῖτε καὶ μὴ ψαύετ᾽, ἀλλ᾽ ἐᾶτέ με
αὐτὸν τὸν ἱερὸν τύμβον ἐξευρεῖν, ἵνα
μοῖρ᾽ ἀνδρὶ τῷδε τῇδε κρυφθῆναι χθονί.
τῇδ᾽ ὧδε, τῇδε βᾶτε· τῇδε γάρ μ᾽ ἄγει
Ἑρμῆς ὁ πομπὸς ἥ τε νερτέρα θεός.
ὦ φῶς ἀφεγγές, πρόσθε πού ποτ᾽ ἦσθ᾽ ἐμόν,
νῦν δ᾽ ἔσχατόν σου τοὐμὸν ἅπτεται δέμας.

no hand to guide me. You must not ever
divulge this place to any mortal man
by revealing its concealed location
or the general area where it lies,
so that for all time it may protect you
more effectively than shields and spears
or many foreign allies. You yourself
will learn, once you enter that place alone,
forbidden things of which no one may speak.
I would not talk of them to any citizen
or to my children, although I love them.
You must always keep these matters secret,
and when your life is coming to an end,
reveal them to your most important heir—
to him alone. He must always pass them on
to his successor. If you keep doing this,
then life in Athens will never be disrupted
by citizens born from the dragon's teeth.[52]
Even if in countless cities men live well,
they find it all too easy to commit
outrageous crimes, for gods are slow to act,
although they clearly intervene when men
abandon piety and turn to madness.[53]
Son of Aegeus, do not let that happen.
But I am stating what you know already.
But since what comes from god urges me on,
let us set off for the designated place
and hesitate no longer.

[OEDIPUS turns his attention to ANTIGONE and ISMENE.]

My children,
follow me, for though it seems new and strange,
I will once more show both of you the way,
just as you two used to guide your father.
So move on. Do not lay a hand on me.
Let me find the sacred burial ground myself,
where Fate has ordained I will lie hidden
here in Athens. This way—follow my lead.
Hermes the Guide and the goddess of the dead,
Persephone, are showing me the path.
O light, that is no light to me, though once,
in earlier days, my eyes could see you,
now for the last time you caress my body.

ἤδη γὰρ ἕρπω τὸν τελευταῖον βίον
κρύψων παρ' Ἅιδην. ἀλλά, φίλτατε ξένων,
αὐτός τε χώρα θ' ἥδε πρόσπολοί τε σοὶ
εὐδαίμονες γένοισθε, κἀπ' εὐπραξίᾳ
μέμνησθέ μου θανόντος εὐτυχεῖς ἀεί.

Χορος

εἰ θέμις ἐστί μοι τὰν ἀφανῆ θεὸν
καὶ σὲ λιταῖς σεβίζειν,
ἐννυχίων ἄναξ,
Αἰδωνεῦ Αἰδωνεῦ, λίσσωμαι
ἄπονα μήτ' ἐπὶ βαρυαχεῖ
ξένον ἐξανύσαι
μόρῳ τὰν παγκευθῆ κάτω
νεκρῶν πλάκα καὶ Στύγιον δόμον.
πολλῶν γὰρ ἂν καὶ μάταν
πημάτων ἱκνουμένων
πάλιν σφε δαίμων δίκαιος αὔξοι.

ὦ χθόνιαι θεαὶ σῶμά τ' ἀνικάτου
θηρός, ὃν ἐν πύλαισι
ταῖσι πολυξένοις
εὐνᾶσθαι κνυζεῖσθαί τ' ἐξ ἄντρων
ἀδάματον φύλακα παρ' Ἀίδᾳ
λόγος αἰὲν ἔχει·
τόν, ὦ Γᾶς παῖ καὶ Ταρτάρου,
κατεύχομαι ἐν καθαρῷ βῆναι
ὁρμωμένῳ νερτέρας
τῷ ξένῳ νεκρῶν πλάκας·
σέ τοι κικλήσκω τὸν αἰένυπνον.

Αγγελος

ἄνδρες πολῖται, ξυντομωτάτως, μὲν ἂν
τύχοιμι λέξας Οἰδίπουν ὀλωλότα·
ἃ δ' ἦν τὰ πραχθέντ', οὔθ' ὁ μῦθος ἐν βραχεῖ
φράσαι πάρεστιν οὔτε τἄργ' ὅσ' ἦν ἐκεῖ.

For already I am shuffling on my way
to hide the final portion of my life
in Hades.

[OEDIPUS stops to address THESEUS.]

But you, most cherished stranger,
may you, your followers, and your land
fare well, and may you, in your prosperity,
remember me, as I move to my death,
and may you have good fortune evermore.

[OEDIPUS, ANTIGONE, ISMENE, and THESEUS move off together.]

CHORUS

If by our traditions it is right
for me to worship with my prayers
the unseen goddess, as well as you,
lord of the dead, then Aidoneus,
O Aidoneus, I entreat you—
may the stranger move on free of pain
or heavy grieving for his fate
to the all-concealing fields of dead
and the chamber of the Styx below.[54]
Through no fault of his own he met
great torments, but may a righteous god
restore his splendour once again.

O goddesses of the lower world
and you, the unconquerable beast,
whose body lies, so people say,
beside the gate of countless guests,
snarling at the entry to your cave,
invincible guardian of Hades,
O child of Earth and Tartarus,
I pray the path the stranger treads
may be left clear, as he moves on
to fields of the dead below.
I cry to you, lord of eternal sleep.[55]

[A MESSENGER enters]

MESSENGER

Citizens, the news I will report is brief—
Oedipus is dead. But I cannot provide
details of his death in a short report,
since what went on there lasted for some time.

ΧΟΡΟΣ

ὄλωλε γὰρ δύστηνος;

ΑΓΓΕΛΟΣ

ὡς λελοιπότα
κεῖνον τὸν ἀεὶ βίοτον ἐξεπίστασο.

ΧΟΡΟΣ

πῶς; ἆρα θείᾳ κἀπόνῳ τάλας τύχῃ;

ΑΓΓΕΛΟΣ

ταῦτ᾽ ἐστὶν ἤδη κἀποθαυμάσαι πρέπον.
ὡς μὲν γὰρ ἐνθένδ᾽ εἷρπε, καὶ σύ που παρὼν
ἔξοισθ᾽, ὑφηγητῆρος οὐδενὸς φίλων,
ἀλλ᾽ αὐτὸς ἡμῖν πᾶσιν ἐξηγούμενος.
ἐπεὶ δ᾽ ἀφῖκτο τὸν καταρράκτην ὀδὸν
χαλκοῖς βάθροισι γῆθεν ἐρριζωμένον,
ἔστη κελεύθων ἐν πολυσχίστων μιᾷ,
κοίλου πέλας κρατῆρος, οὗ τὰ Θησέως
Περίθου τε κεῖται πίστ᾽ ἀεὶ ξυνθήματα.
ἀφ᾽ οὗ μέσος στὰς τοῦ τε Θορικίου πέτρου
κοίλης τ᾽ ἀχέρδου κἀπὸ λαΐνου τάφου,
καθέζετ᾽· εἶτ᾽ ἔλυσε δυσπινεῖς στολάς.
κἄπειτ᾽ ἀΰσας παῖδας ἠνώγει ῥυτῶν
ὑδάτων ἐνεγκεῖν λουτρὰ καὶ χοάς ποθεν·
τὼ δ᾽ εὐχλόου Δήμητρος εἰς προσόψιον
πάγον μολοῦσαι τάσδ᾽ ἐπιστολὰς πατρὶ
ταχεῖ ᾽πόρευσαν σὺν χρόνῳ, λουτροῖς τέ νιν
ἐσθῆτί τ᾽ ἐξήσκησαν ᾗ νομίζεται.
ἐπεὶ δὲ παντὸς εἶχε δρῶντος ἡδονὴν
κοὐκ ἦν ἔτ᾽ οὐδὲν ἀργὸν ὧν ἐφίετο,
κτύπησε μὲν Ζεὺς χθόνιος αἱ δὲ παρθένοι
ῥίγησαν, ὡς ἤκουσαν· ἐς δὲ γούνατα
πατρὸς πεσοῦσαι ᾽κλαιον οὐδ᾽ ἀνίεσαν
στέρνων ἀραγμοὺς οὐδὲ παμμήκεις γόους.

CHORUS
Has the unlucky man died at last?

MESSENGER
You can rest assured—he has left this life.

CHORUS
How did the poor man die? Was his passing
divinely ordered and free of pain?

MESSENGER
To tell the truth,
his death inspired wonder. How he left here
you already know, since you were present.
None of his loved ones led him on his way.
Instead, he acted as a guide for all of us.
When he came to the steep cleft that plunges
down the bronze stairway rooted deep in earth,
he stopped near one of the many pathways
which converge by a hollow in the rock
where Theseus and Peirithous set up
the lasting pledge of their eternal bond.
He stood halfway between the basin there
and the Thorician rock, with the stone tomb
and the hollow pear tree on either side.[56]
There he sat down, took off his filthy clothes,
and, after calling for his daughters, asked them
to bring him water from a flowing stream,
so he could wash and offer a libation.
The two of them went up the rocky hill
of fresh, green Demeter, which we could see,
soon came back with what their father wanted,
and then, following our usual customs,
washed and dressed him.[57] When they were finished
and had done all that Oedipus requested,
without ignoring any of his wishes,
at that moment Zeus of the Underworld
produced a peal of thunder.[58] The young girls
heard the noise and trembled. Then they collapsed,
falling at their father's knees and weeping.
They kept on striking their breasts and wailing,
voicing their pain with loud and bitter cries.

ὁ δ᾽ ὡς ἀκούει φθόγγον ἐξαίφνης πικρόν,
πτύξας ἐπ᾽ αὐταῖς χεῖρας εἶπεν· ὦ τέκνα,
οὐκ ἔστ᾽ ἔθ᾽ ὑμῖν τῇδ᾽ ἐν ἡμέρᾳ πατήρ.
ὄλωλε γὰρ δὴ πάντα τἀμά, κοὐκέτι
τὴν δυσπόνητον ἕξετ᾽ ἀμφ᾽ ἐμοὶ τροφήν·
σκληρὰν μέν, οἶδα, παῖδες· ἀλλ᾽ ἓν γὰρ μόνον
τὰ πάντα λύει ταῦτ᾽ ἔπος μοχθήματα.
τὸ γὰρ φιλεῖν οὐκ ἔστιν ἐξ ὅτου πλέον
ἢ τοῦδε τἀνδρὸς ἔσχεθ᾽, οὗ τητώμεναι
τὸ λοιπὸν ἤδη τὸν βίον διάζετον.
τοιαῦτ᾽ ἐπ᾽ ἀλλήλοισιν ἀμφικείμενοι
λύγδην ἔκλαιον πάντες. ὡς δὲ πρὸς τέλος
γόων ἀφίκοντ᾽ οὐδ᾽ ἔτ᾽ ὠρώρει βοή,
ἦν μὲν σιωπή· φθέγμα δ᾽ ἐξαίφνης τινὸς
θώϋξεν αὐτόν, ὥστε πάντας ὀρθίας
στῆσαι φόβῳ δείσαντας ἐξαίφνης τρίχας,
καλεῖ γὰρ αὐτὸν πολλὰ πολλαχῇ θεός·
ὦ οὗτος οὗτος, Οἰδίπους, τί μέλλομεν
χωρεῖν; πάλαι δὴ τἀπὸ σοῦ βραδύνεται.
ὁ δ᾽ ὡς ἐπῄσθετ᾽ ἐκ θεοῦ καλούμενος,
αὐδᾷ μολεῖν οἱ γῆς ἄνακτα Θησέα.
κἀπεὶ προσῆλθεν, εἶπεν· ὦ φίλον κάρα,
δός μοι χερὸς σῆς πίστιν ὁρκίαν τέκνοις,
ὑμεῖς τε, παῖδες, τῷδε· καὶ καταίνεσον
μήποτε προδώσειν τάσδ᾽ ἑκών, τελεῖν δ᾽ ὅσ᾽ ἂν
μέλλῃς φρονῶν εὖ ξυμφέροντ᾽ αὐτοῖς ἀεί.
ὁ δ᾽, ὡς ἀνὴρ γενναῖος, οὐκ οἴκτου μέτα
κατῄνεσεν τάδ᾽ ὅρκιος δράσειν ξένῳ.
ὅπως δὲ ταῦτ᾽ ἔδρασεν, εὐθὺς Οἰδίπους
ψαύσας ἀμαυραῖς χερσὶν ὧν παίδων λέγει·
'ὦ παῖδε, τλάσας χρὴ τὸ γενναῖον φρενὶ
χωρεῖν τόπων ἐκ τῶνδε, μηδ᾽ ἃ μὴ θέμις

When he heard these sudden howls of sorrow,
Oedipus held them in his arms and said,
"Children, today your father is no more.
Everything I was has perished, and you two
will no longer share the heavy burden
of looking after me. Children, I know
that task was difficult, but a single word
makes up for all your labours, for never
will you find anyone whose love for you
is greater than the love you both received
from the man who was your father. And now,
for all the days remaining in your lives,
you will not have him with you anymore."
They remained like this, holding one another,
all of them distraught with grief and sobbing.
Then they paused and stopped their mournful wailing.
They made no sound, and everything was still.
Suddenly a voice called out to Oedipus.
It made the hairs on all our heads stand up—
we were so terrified! Again and again
the god cried out to him in different ways,
"You there, you, Oedipus, why this delay
in our departure? You have been lingering
for far too long." Once he became aware
the god was summoning him, Oedipus
asked lord Theseus to come up to him,
and when the king did so, Oedipus said,
"My dear friend, give me the time-honoured pledge
of your right hand for my children, and you,
my daughters, give him your sworn pledge, as well.
My lord, promise you will not betray them
of your own free will but will always do
whatever you believe is best for them."
Since Theseus is an honorable king,
he showed no sign of sorrow and agreed
to fulfil that promise for the stranger.
Once Theseus had sworn he would do this,
Oedipus suddenly clutched his daughters
with his blind hands and said to them, "Children,
you must bear my death with a noble heart
and leave this place. For you cannot believe

λεύσσειν δικαιοῦν μηδὲ φωνούντων κλύειν,
ἀλλ᾽ ἕρπεθ᾽ ὡς τάχιστα· πλὴν ὁ κύριος
Θησεὺς παρέστω μανθάνων τὰ δρώμενα.᾽
τοσαῦτα φωνήσαντος εἰσηκούσαμεν
ξύμπαντες· ἀστακτὶ δὲ σὺν ταῖς παρθένοις
στένοντες ὡμαρτοῦμεν. ὡς δ᾽ ἀπήλθομεν,
χρόνῳ βραχεῖ στραφέντες ἐξαπείδομεν
τὸν ἄνδρα τὸν μὲν οὐδαμοῦ παρόντ᾽ ἔτι,
ἄνακτα δ᾽ αὐτὸν ὀμμάτων ἐπίσκιον
χεῖρ᾽ ἀντέχοντα κρατός, ὡς δεινοῦ τινος
φόβου φανέντος οὐδ᾽ ἀνασχετοῦ βλέπειν.
ἔπειτα μέντοι βαιὸν οὐδὲ σὺν χρόνῳ
ὁρῶμεν αὐτὸν γῆν τε προσκυνοῦνθ᾽ ἅμα
καὶ τὸν θεῶν Ὄλυμπον ἐν ταὐτῷ λόγῳ.
μόρῳ δ᾽ ὁποίῳ κεῖνος ὤλετ᾽, οὐδ᾽ ἂν εἷς
θνητῶν φράσειε, πλὴν τὸ Θησέως κάρα.
οὐ γάρ τις αὐτὸν οὔτε πυρφόρος θεοῦ
κεραυνὸς ἐξέπραξεν οὔτε ποντία
θύελλα κινηθεῖσα τῷ τότ᾽ ἐν χρόνῳ,
ἀλλ᾽ ἤ τις ἐκ θεῶν πομπὸς ἢ τὸ νερτέρων
εὔνουν διαστὰν γῆς ἀλύπητον βάθρον.
ἁνὴρ γὰρ οὐ στενακτὸς οὐδὲ σὺν νόσοις
ἀλγεινὸς ἐξεπέμπετ᾽, ἀλλ᾽ εἴ τις βροτῶν
θαυμαστός. εἰ δὲ μὴ δοκῶ φρονῶν λέγειν,
οὐκ ἂν παρείμην οἷσι μὴ δοκῶ φρονεῖν.

Χορος

ποῦ δ᾽ αἵ τε παῖδες χοἰ προπέμψαντες φίλων;

Αγγελος

αἵδ᾽ οὐχ ἑκάς· γόων γὰρ οὐκ ἀσήμονες
φθόγγοι σφε σημαίνουσι δεῦρ᾽ ὁρμωμένας.

it is appropriate to view those acts
which our traditions say should not be seen
or listen to things said you should not hear.
You must go now—and quickly. Let Theseus,
the sovereign king, stay and learn what happens."
All of us heard him say these words and then,
full of sorrow, with our eyes streaming tears,
we followed the young girls and left the place.
Once we moved off, after a few moments
we looked back from a distance and noticed
Oedipus was no longer to be seen.
Theseus was alone, holding his hands up
right before his face to protect his eyes,
as if he had just seen something fearful
that no human being could bear to see.
And then, after that, a short time later,
we saw Theseus offering a single prayer,
worshipping divine Olympus and the Earth.
How Oedipus met his fate and perished
no mortal knows, other than Theseus.
It was no fiery lightning bolt from god
that took him away, nor was he carried off
by some momentary whirlwind rising
out at sea. No—some escort from the gods
came for him or else, in an act of kindness,
the rock-hard world of the dead split open
so he would feel no pain. He passed away
without a groan or symptom of disease.
If any mortal man has ever died
in a miraculous way, then he did.
If someone thinks I talk just like a fool,
I will not try to teach him otherwise,
since he believes my words do not make sense.

Chorus
Where are the ones who went away with him—
his daughters and their friends?

Messenger
Not far away. The sound of their laments
is getter closer—they are almost here.

[ANTIGONE and ISMENE enter]

ΑΝΤΙΓΟΝΗ

αἰαῖ, φεῦ, ἔστιν ἔστι νῷν δὴ
οὐ τὸ μέν, ἄλλο δὲ μή, πατρὸς ἔμφυτον
ἄλαστον αἷμα δυσμόροιν στενάζειν,
ᾧτινι τὸν πολὺν
ἄλλοτε μὲν πόνον ἔμπεδον εἴχομεν,
ἐν πυμάτῳ δ᾽ ἀλόγιστα παροίσομεν
ἰδόντε καὶ παθόντε.

ΧΟΡΟΣ

τί δ᾽ ἔστιν;

ΑΝΤΙΓΟΝΗ

ἔστιν μὲν εἰκάσαι, φίλοι.

ΧΟΡΟΣ

βέβηκεν;

ΑΝΤΙΓΟΝΗ

ὡς μάλιστ᾽ ἂν ἐν πόθῳ λάβοις.
τί γάρ, ὅτῳ μήτ᾽ Ἄρης
μήτε πόντος ἀντέκυρσεν,
ἄσκοποι δὲ πλάκες ἔμαρψαν
ἐν ἀφανεῖ τινι μόρῳ φερόμενον.
τάλαινα· νῷν δ᾽ ὀλεθρία
νὺξ ἐπ᾽ ὄμμασιν βέβακε. πῶς γὰρ ἤ τιν᾽ ἀπίαν
γᾶν ἢ πόντιον κλύδων᾽ ἀλώμεναι, βίου
δύσοιστον ἕξομεν τροφάν;

ΙΣΜΗΝΗ

οὐ κάτοιδα. κατά με φόνιος Ἀΐδας ἕλοι
πατρὶ ξυνθανεῖν γεραιῷ
τάλαιναν, ὡς ἔμοιγ᾽ ὁ μέλλων βίος οὐ βιωτός.

ΧΟΡΟΣ

ὦ διδύμα τέκνων ἀρίστα, τὸ φέρον ἐκ θεοῦ φέρειν,
μηδὲν ἄγαν φλέγεσθον· οὔ τοι κατάμεμπτ᾽ ἔβητον.

ANTIGONE
Alas! This is so sad! Now the two of us,
both subject to an abject destiny,
will spend every moment grieving
the family curse we carry in our blood,
inherited from our father. For him
before today we laboured long and hard.
Now he is dead, and we are left to speak
of what we saw and went through at the end,
events that baffle reason.

CHORUS
What happened?

ANTIGONE
One can only guess, my friends.

CHORUS
Has Oedipus truly gone?

ANTIGONE
He has gone
exactly as one might have wished—
not seized by Ares, god of war,
or by the sea, but snatched away
by unseen fate and carried off
to the hidden fields of death.
I feel so sad! A death-filled night
now shrouds our eyes. How do we find
daily nourishment in a harsh life
of wandering some distant land
or roaming waves of the sea?

ISMENE
I do not know.
Things are desperate! How I wish
Hades the killer would seize me too
and let me share death with my old father!
For the life I face is not worth living.

CHORUS
You two most excellent of daughters
must bear whatever gods provide.
Do not let your hearts burn up
in flames of excess passion—
for what has happened to you here
gives you no reason to complain.

ΑΝΤΙΓΟΝΗ

πόθος τοὶ καὶ κακῶν ἄρ᾽ ἦν τις.
καὶ γὰρ ὃ μηδαμὰ δὴ φίλον ἦν φίλον,
ὁπότε γε καὶ τὸν ἐν χεροῖν κατεῖχον.
ὦ πάτερ, ὦ φίλος,
ὦ τὸν ἀεὶ κατὰ γᾶς σκότον εἱμένος·
οὐδέ γ᾽ ἔνερθ᾽ ἀφίλητος ἐμοί ποτε
καὶ τᾷδε μὴ κυρήσῃς.

ΧΟΡΟΣ

ἔπραξεν;

ΑΝΤΙΓΟΝΗ

ἔπραξεν οἷον ἤθελεν.

ΧΟΡΟΣ

τὸ ποῖον;

ΑΝΤΙΓΟΝΗ

ἇς ἔχρῃζε γᾶς ἐπὶ ξένας
ἔθανε· κοίταν δ᾽ ἔχει
νέρθεν εὐσκίαστον αἰέν,
οὐδὲ πένθος ἔλιπ᾽ ἄκλαυτον.
ἀνὰ γὰρ ὄμμα σε τόδ᾽, ὦ πάτερ, ἐμὸν
στένει δακρῦον, οὐδ᾽ ἔχω
πῶς με χρὴ τὸ σὸν τάλαιναν ἀφανίσαι τοσόνδ᾽ ἄχος.
ὤμοι, γᾶς ἐπὶ ξένας θανεῖν ἔχρῃζες ἀλλ᾽
ἔρημος ἔθανες ὧδέ μοι.

ΙΣΜΗΝΗ

ὦ τάλαινα, τίς ἄρα με πότμος αὖθις ὧδ᾽
< . . . >
ἐπαμμένει σέ τ᾽, ὦ φίλα, τὰς πατρὸς ὧδ᾽ ἐρήμας;

ΧΟΡΟΣ

ἀλλ᾽ ἐπεὶ ὀλβίως γ᾽ ἔλυσεν τὸ τέλος, ὦ φίλαι, βίου,
λήγετε τοῦδ᾽ ἄχους· κακῶν γὰρ δυσάλωτος οὐδείς.

ANTIGONE

One laments the loss of even painful things.
That life for which I felt no love at all
I did love when I held him in my arms.
O my beloved father, now wrapped
in the underworld's eternal darkness,
even though you are no longer here,
my sister and I will love you always.

CHORUS

He ended . . .

ANTIGONE

He had the end he wished for.

CHORUS

In what way?

ANTIGONE

He perished in a foreign land,
as he desired, and is eternally at rest
beneath the ground in a well-shaded place.
He did not leave us without being mourned.
With tear-filled eyes I still grieve for you,
my father, and in my unhappy state
I do not know how I should relieve
the grief I feel with such intensity.
Alas! You wished to die in a strange land,
but when you died I was not with you!

ISMENE

I feel so desperate! What fate awaits us,
my dear sister, now we have no father?[59]

CHORUS

Friends, since the ending of his life was blessed,
you should cease this grieving. No mortal
has a life immune from great misfortune.

ΑΝΤΙΓΟΝΗ

πάλιν, φίλα, συθῶμεν.

ΙΣΜΗΝΗ

ὡς τί ῥέξομεν;

ΑΝΤΙΓΟΝΗ

ἵμερος ἔχει με.

ΙΣΜΗΝΗ

τίς;

ΑΝΤΙΓΟΝΗ

τὰν χθόνιον ἑστίαν ἰδεῖν

ΙΣΜΗΝΗ

τίνος;

ΑΝΤΙΓΟΝΗ

πατρός, τάλαιν᾽ ἐγώ.

ΙΣΜΗΝΗ

θέμις δὲ πῶς τάδ᾽ ἐστί; μῶν
οὐχ ὁρᾷς;

ΑΝΤΙΓΟΝΗ

τί τόδε ἐπέπληξας;

ΙΣΜΗΝΗ

καὶ τόδ᾽, ὡς

ΑΝΤΙΓΟΝΗ

τί τόδε μάλ᾽ αὖθις;

ΙΣΜΗΝΗ

ἄταφος ἔπιτνε δίχα τε παντός.

ΑΝΤΙΓΟΝΗ

ἄγε με, καὶ τότ᾽ ἐπενάριξον.

ΙΣΜΗΝΗ

αἰαῖ, δυστάλαινα, ποῦ δῆτ᾽
αὖθις ὧδ᾽ ἔρημος ἄπορος
αἰῶνα τλάμον᾽ ἕξω;

ANTGONE
Dear sister, we must hurry back.

ISMENE
But why?
What do we have to do?

ANTIGONE
I need to see it!

ISMENE
See what?

ANTIGONE
That earthly resting place.

ISMENE
Whose resting place?

ANTIGONE
I cannot bear this grief—
I have to see our father's burial ground!

ISMENE
But how does such a wish not break our laws?
Don't you see that?

ANTIGONE
Why do you disapprove?

ISMENE
And then there is also this . . .

ANTIGONE
What other things
are you complaining of?

ISMENE
Our father perished
without a grave—and no one else was there.

ANTIGONE
Lead me there, and then slaughter me, as well.[60]

ISMENE
Alas for me, in my miserable state!
Where am I now to spend this wretched life,
with no support and totally abandoned!

Χορος
φίλαι, τρέσητε μηδέν.

Αντιγονη
ἀλλὰ ποῖ φύγω;

Χορος
καὶ πάρος ἀπέφυγε

Αντιγονη
τί;

Χορος
τὰ σφῷν τὸ μὴ πίτνειν κακῶς.

Αντιγονη
φρονῶ.

Χορος
τί δῆθ' ὅπερ νοεῖς;

Αντιγονη
ὅπως μολούμεθ' ἐς δόμους
οὐκ ἔχω.

Χορος
μηδέ γε μάτευε.

Αντιγονη
μόγος ἔχει.

Χορος
καὶ πάρος ἐπεῖχε.

Αντιγονη
τοτὲ μὲν ἄπορα, τοτὲ δ' ὕπερθεν.

Χορος
μέγ' ἄρα πέλαγος ἐλάχετόν τι.

Αντιγονη
ναὶ ναί.

Χορος
ξύμφημι καὐτός.

CHORUS
Do not fear, my friends.

ANTIGONE
But where do I take refuge?[61]

CHORUS
You have already found a place for that.

ANTIGONE
What are you saying?

CHORUS
You two have reached
a place where you are safe from harm.

ANTIGONE
Yes, I understand that.

CHORUS
What else is there?
What are you thinking?

ANTIGONE
I have no idea
how we get home to Thebes.

CHORUS
Don't even think of that!

ANTIGONE
This present trouble has us in its grip!

CHORUS
The evils you faced before were harsh enough.

ANTIGONE
Back then we had no hope. Now things are worse.

CHORUS
You have been destined for a sea of troubles.

ANTIGONE
Yes, that is true.

CHORUS
That's what it seems to me.

ΑΝΤΙΓΟΝΗ

αἰαῖ, ποῖ μόλωμεν, ὦ Ζεῦ;
ἐλπίδων γὰρ ἐς τίν' ἔτι με
δαίμων τανῦν γ' ἐλαύνει;

ΘΗΣΕΥΣ

παύετε θρήνων, παῖδες· ἐν οἷς γὰρ
χάρις ἡ χθονία ξύν' ἀπόκειται,
πενθεῖν οὐ χρή· νέμεσις γάρ.

ΑΝΤΙΓΟΝΗ

ὦ τέκνον Αἰγέως, προσπίτνομέν σοι.

ΘΗΣΕΥΣ

τίνος, ὦ παῖδες, χρείας ἀνύσαι;

ΑΝΤΙΓΟΝΗ

τύμβον θέλομεν προσιδεῖν αὐταὶ
πατρὸς ἡμετέρου.

ΘΗΣΕΥΣ

ἀλλ' οὐ θεμιτόν.

ΑΝΤΙΓΟΝΗ

πῶς εἶπας, ἄναξ, κοίραν' Ἀθηνῶν;

ΘΗΣΕΥΣ

ὦ παῖδες, ἀπεῖπεν ἐμοὶ κεῖνος
μήτε πελάζειν ἐς τούσδε τόπους
μήτ' ἐπιφωνεῖν μηδένα θνητῶν
θήκην ἱεράν, ἣν κεῖνος ἔχει.
καὶ ταῦτά μ' ἔφη πράσσοντα καλῶς
χώραν ἕξειν αἰὲν ἄλυπον.
ταῦτ' οὖν ἔκλυεν δαίμων ἡμῶν
χὡ πάντ' ἀΐων Διὸς Ὅρκος.

ΑΝΤΙΓΟΝΗ

ἀλλ' εἰ τάδ' ἔχει κατὰ νοῦν κείνῳ,
ταῦτ' ἂν ἀπαρκοῖ· Θήβας δ' ἡμᾶς

ANTIGONE
Alas! Alas! O Zeus, where do we go?
Where is our destiny now driving us—
towards what last remaining hope?

[Enter THESEUS]

THESEUS
Stop these laments, children! When gods below
store up public favours for the dead,
we must feel no sorrow—for if we do
then retribution follows.[62]

ANTIGONE
Son of Aegeus,
we beg one request from you.

THESEUS
What is it,
my children. What do you desire?

ANTIGONE
We wish
to see our father's grave with our own eyes.

THESEUS
To go there is forbidden by our laws.

ANTIGONE
O lord and ruler of Athenians,
what do you mean?

THESEUS
Children, your father told me
that no living person should come near the place
or speak any words beside the sacred ground
where he is buried. And he promised me,
if I made sure of that, then I would keep
the land of Athens free of pain forever.
The god there heard me swear that I would do it,
and so did Horkos, too, Zeus' servant,
who witnesses all oaths and makes them strong.[63]

ANTIGONE
If this is what my father has in mind,
then we must comply. Send us on our way

τὰς ὠγυγίους πέμψον, ἐάν πως
διακωλύσωμεν ἰόντα φόνον
τοῖσιν ὁμαίμοις.

Θησευς

δράσω καὶ τάδε καὶ πάνθ᾽ ὁπόσ᾽ ἂν
μέλλω πράσσειν πρόσφορά θ᾽ ὑμῖν
καὶ τῷ κατὰ γῆς, ὃς νέον ἔρρει,
πρὸς χάριν· οὐ δεῖ μ᾽ ἀποκάμνειν.

Χορος

ἀλλ᾽ ἀποπαύετε μηδ᾽ ἐπὶ πλείω
θρῆνον ἐγείρετε·
πάντως γὰρ ἔχει τάδε κῦρος.

to ancient Thebes, to see if we somehow
can stop the coming slaughter of our brothers.

THESEUS

I will do that and perform whatever else
may be a service to you and to the man
who has just died and lies beneath the earth.
On his behalf I must spare no effort,
for Oedipus has earned my gratitude.

CHORUS

So let us cease with our laments,
and chant our funeral songs no more.
For these events have all been preordained.

NOTES

1. The Eumenides (Kindly Ones) is another name for the Furies, the goddesses of blood revenge, especially within the family. The Greeks sometimes liked to give particularly fearful things euphemistic names (e.g., calling the Black Sea the Euxine or "Hospitable" Sea).

2. As we learn shortly, Apollo has told Oedipus that when he reaches a holy shrine his wanderings will end. See line 106 ff. below.

3. The Titans, descendants of Earth and Sky, were divine figures of the generation before the Olympians. Prometheus, son of the Titan Iapetus, stole fire from heaven and gave it to human beings.

4. Jebb explains that near this sacred grove was a steep channel in the rock, where someone had constructed some bronze steps. It was called the "threshold of Hades." Hence the whole area was called "the bronze threshold" and was considered an important element in the safety of Athens.

5. Some commentators have suggested that there may well be a statue of Colonus somewhere on the stage. If so, this line would presumably be a reference to it.

6. Libations to the Furies were made, not with wine, but with water.

7. As Jebb points out, this remark is bitterly ironic. Oedipus is, in effect, saying: "I have suffered more than any other living person, but perhaps I have not yet suffered enough to win a concession from the gods."

8. In the religious rituals libations of water and of water mixed with honey were poured separately.

9. At this point there is a gap in the manuscript of three or four lines.

10. Laius was Oedipus' father; Labdacus was the father of Laius. They were both kings of Thebes.

11. Earlier the Chorus promised Oedipus he would not be removed from refuge against his will.

12. The argument here is that Oedipus earlier deceived the Chorus by not revealing who he was before they made their promise to him. Therefore, they are justified in setting that promise aside.

13. Oedipus is arguing that in his actions he was responding to the treatment he received from his parents (who had tried to kill him as an infant by exposing him on Mount Cithaeron, outside Thebes). And in attacking his father, Oedipus was reacting to the latter's hostile actions. Hence, even if he had known that his opponent was his father, Oedipus states, one could not consider him evil for defending himself.

14. This is almost certainly a reference to the way his parents tried to kill the infant Oedipus by pinning his feet together and abandoning him on the mountain. They were driven to do that by a prophecy that said the newborn child would grow up to kill his father.

15. Ismene presumably enters on foot, having dismounted from her horse.

16. The curse on the family of Laius, Oedipus' father, originated in Laius' abduction and rape of Chrysippus, a young son of Pelops, king of Pisa (in the Peloponnese) and Pelops' host. As a result of this crime, Chrysippus committed suicide, and Pelops laid a curse on Laius and his descendants. A profane act by a member of the family could bring religious pollution to an entire community.

17. Sophocles here makes Polyneices the elder of the two brothers. In some other versions of the story, Eteocles is the firstborn son. This change makes each brother a wrongdoer: Eteocles for usurping his elder brother, and Polyneices for seeking a foreign army to fight against his homeland.

18. Polyneices married Argeia, daughter of Adrastus, king of Argos, as part of his strategy to raise an army and attack Thebes.

19. This sentence is rather ambiguous in the Greek. If Argos defeats Thebes, Polyneices and his friends will win honour. The alternative is that Argos will sing someone's praises to the skies. Jebb suggests that Argos will be singing the praises of Thebes for having won the battle. Another possibility is that Argos will be exalting Polyneices and his friends for having taken a great risk, fought the battle, and behaved heroically, even though they did not succeed. The latter seems to me more probable, given that it is the sort of idea young men bent on a dangerous expedition would come up with. Cadmean land is a reference to Thebes: Cadmus was the one who founded the city.

20. Oedipus' anger at his sons is not primarily rage at their foolish conduct for quarrelling over the throne but rather fury because, although the sons know about the prophecy that the security of Thebes is to depend upon the way Thebans treat Oedipus and his tomb, they are not working to get him accepted back at Thebes and perhaps even restored to the throne. Instead they are concentrating on trying to become king themselves. His concern is the injury he thinks has been done to him. What the latest prophecy is saying is that if Oedipus is buried in Athenian lands then, at some point in the future the Thebans will invade those lands but will be defeated by the Athenians at Oedipus' grave. In other words, Oedipus' anger will eventually work against them. The only way of averting that is to get control of Oedipus now, to make sure he cannot be buried in Athens.

21. It is not clear how long a period of time passed between Oedipus' self-mutilation and his exile from Thebes. During this period the city was ruled by Creon, who presumably made the decision to exile Oedipus.

22. Oedipus has spoken earlier about a prophecy he received from Apollo many years before that he would finally find rest (see line 106 above). He is now combining that oracular utterance with what Ismene has told him about recent prophecies concerning him.

23. As Jebb observes, the Chorus' shock here suggests that they are just finding out that Jocasta was not only Oedipus' wife and mother, but also the mother of his children. In some versions of the story of Oedipus, he had no children with Jocasta, and his children were from a second wife, Euryganeia.

24. Thebes had been plagued by a monster, the Sphinx, which could only be conquered by someone who answered a riddle correctly. Oedipus solved the riddle and saved the city. He was made king for his services and married Jocasta, the wife of king Laius (who had been murdered some years before).

25. Oedipus killed his father, Laius when the two encountered each other in a place where three roads meet. Laius and his escort shoved Oedipus aside and assaulted him. Thinking his life in danger, Oedipus killed them all, not knowing who they were.

26. Theseus, one of the most famous legendary heroes of Athens, was the son of Aethra, daughter of king Pittheus of Troezen. His father was Aegeus, king of Athens. After Theseus was conceived in Troezen, his father returned to Athens, but he left behind evidence of his identity

for his son to discover when he was old enough. Theseus grew up in Troezen and learned about his father as a young man. He set off for Athens and after a series of famous adventures was eventually reunited with Aegeus, his father.

27. Theseus seems surprised by Oedipus' remarks, since he is probably assuming Oedipus will request protection during his lifetime. Oedipus, however, is concerned only about where he will be buried; hence, he does not care about what happens to him between now and his death, so long as he is confident his grave will be in Athens. As we soon learn, Oedipus' request to be buried in Athens implicitly includes a demand that the Athenians will not hand him over to anyone else, because if he is taken away, then Theseus will be unable to fulfil his pledge to bury Oedipus at Athens.

28. The nymphs of Mount Nysa were given the infant god Dionysus to raise after he was born from Zeus' thigh. They later became the first of those who joined him in his revels (the Bacchantes).

29. The two great goddesses are Demeter and her daughter Persephone. Persephone was gathering a narcissus when she was abducted by Hades, god of the underworld.

30. The "great Dorian isle of Pelops" is a reference to the Peloponnese, that area of mainland Greece south of the Isthmus of Corinth (it is almost an island). Jebb notes that Sophocles does not mean that the olive tree does not grow elsewhere, but rather that the olive does not flourish in other places the way it does in Athens, where it enjoys divine protection. The tree was, according to Athenian legends, a gift from the goddess Athena, who made the first one spring spontaneously from the soil of the city (hence human beings did not plant it in Athens).

31. Zeus here is called "morios," is a word referring to the sacred olive trees in Athens, of which Zeus was the divine guardian. Hence, the title Zeus Morios.

32. Nereus, a sea god in Greek mythology, was a son of Pontus and Gaia (the Sea and the Earth) and the father of the fifty Nereids, nymphs who lived in the sea. This last stanza is a tribute to the importance of Poseidon at Athens. According to legend he introduced horses in Athens and helped to make Athenians expert sailors.

33. Creon was the brother of Oedipus' wife and mother, Jocasta.

34. The word "justly" here refers to the law. Creon is reminding those listening that Thebes has a better legal claim to Oedipus than Athens does, because of the time Oedipus spent there and his family connection with Creon.

35. Creon's appeal for the Chorus to witness Oedipus's conduct is a continuation of his legal thinking. Oedipus wishes to associate himself with Colonus and Athens. Creon has been making the point that, given Oedipus' history and family ties, Thebes has a better legal right to have Oedipus back. At this point, seeing that neither Oedipus nor the Chorus is accepting the legal argument, Creon resorts to threats and violence.

36. The "triumph" Creon refers to is Oedipus' "victory" in not returning to Thebes with him. Creon is claiming here that he has been acting in the best interests of Thebes and of Oedipus' family, although, as absolute ruler of the city, he has no need to defer to their wishes. He is also pointing out that Oedipus' temper has always led to consequences injurious to his family (e.g., his own self-mutilation and expulsion from Thebes, the suicide of Jocasta, his mother-wife and Creon's sister, and the harsh life of his two daughters).

37. The Hill of Ares is a rocky outcrop near the entrance to the Acropolis in Athens. The Council there, the Areopagus, was a court dealing with criminal and civil cases and general moral censorship in the earlier days of Athenian democracy.

38. Theseus is apparently assuming that Creon has entered into a secret agreement with some unspecified Athenian conspirators before challenging Theseus' royal authority by entering his territory. There is no mention of that elsewhere in the play or in other versions of the story.

39. The Chorus is here imagining the impending clash between Theseus and Creon, which, in their view, may take place either on the bay of Eleusis ("the Pythian shores") or else at Eleusis, the centre of a major religious festival dedicated to the goddess Demeter ("beside the torch-lit shore"). In the next section they consider a third possibility. Ares is the god of war, and the goddesses referred to are Demeter and her daughter Persephone. The Eumolpidae were the priests of the religious rituals, responsible for ensuring the secrets of the divine mysteries.

40. This tribute to the two main deities of Athens, Athena and Poseidon, identifies the former with the epithet *hippeia* ("of the horse," "equestrian"), an association linked to her as the inventor of the

chariot, and the latter by a common epithet "encircling the earth" and by a reference to his mother, Rhea, also the mother of the gods Zeus and Hades.

41. These lines indicate that Oedipus still feels he is suffering from religious pollution. Hence, anyone who shows him affection (e.g., by touching) runs the risk of being contaminated. Those who have been with him throughout his suffering run no such risk, since they have long been in frequent physical contact with him.

42. Antigone's obvious point here is that in his past actions Oedipus has let his explosive temper take control of his actions, with disastrous effect. The most obvious evidence for that is his self-inflicted blindness.

43. The words *Dorian* and *Apian* in these lines both refer to the Peloponnese. The word *Argos* by itself can refer to a number of different places in ancient Hellas.

44. Eteoclus, the Argive leader in the force Polyneices has assembled, should obviously not be confused with Eteocles, Polyneices' brother. The name Parthenopaeus means "child of the maiden" or "child of the virgin."

45. Polyneices words mean, in effect, "I am your son, but if I am not (because you have disowned me), then I am the child of fate, even if among the general public I am still considered your child."

46. This detail seems to contradict the chronology of events concerning the governance of Thebes. According to lines 400 ff. above, after Oedipus blinded himself, his sons deferred to the authority of Creon, who ruled as regent, and it seems they began their fight after Oedipus went into exile. Creon himself speaks as if he has sole regal authority in Thebes, but we are told (by Polyneices and Oedipus) that Eteocles is now the ruling king. There has been no suggestion up to this point that Polyneices was ever *de facto* king of Thebes, although, as he says, he is the elder son and therefore, in his eyes, the rightful heir.

47. Jebb offers the useful note that curses, once uttered, become divine agents of vengeance. Oedipus is therefore calling for the agents created by his earlier curses against his two sons to come to his assistance now.

48. Oedipus is claiming here that his curse on Polyneices will defeat any legal claims Polyneices may have to justify his attack on Thebes (both as a suppliant and as the elder son) because ancient natural Justice demands that children respect their parents, a law that is more powerful than any Polyneices can appeal to.

49. Tartarus is a deep pit in Hades, usually associated with punishment and imprisonment. The word "paternal" may refer to the idea that darkness the father of everything or that Polyneices will be going to a place as dark as the world of his father, Oedipus.

50. These lines from the Chorus refer once again to the notion that contact with a polluted person (i.e., someone cursed by the gods) can bring the anger of the gods down on those who have had dealings with him.

51. For details of what Oedipus has promised Theseus, see lines 723 ff. above.

52. The founder of Thebes, Cadmus, killed a dragon living at the site of the future city. When he sowed the monster's teeth across the earth, armed men sprang up and began fighting and killing each other, until only a few were left. These men were the first Thebans. Oedipus is, in effect, promising that Athens will never suffer from civil disturbances, if Athenians remember his instructions.

53. The point here is that even well-governed cities will suffer from the hubristic ambitions of some citizens because, although the gods will eventually punish evil citizens, such divine retribution is slow and therefore the troublemakers will have time to disrupt civic life.

54. Aidoneus is another name for Hades, god of the underworld. The "unseen goddess" is Persephone, wife of Hades. The name "Styx" refers to the river separating the earth and the underworld. The word also often designates the underworld generally.

55. The "goddesses in the lower world" are probably the Furies, the divine agents of blood revenge, and the "beast" is a reference to Cerberus, a dog with several heads (the number varies from one account to another) who is a resident of Hades, with a lair near the entrance to the underworld. It is not clear to whom the phrase "child of Earth and Tartarus" refers, since it does not describe the parentage of Cerberus (perhaps it is a general reference to Death, the "lord of eternal sleep").

56. For an explanation of the "bronze stairway" as the threshold of the descent to Hades, see Endnote 4 above. Peirithous was king of the Lapiths and a close friend of Theseus. In a famous heroic exploit, the two men together went down to Hades, were captured by Hades, and then rescued by Hercules. The "lasting pledge" is some sort of memorial to their friendship. Thoricus was a town in Attica. Jebb notes that in a legendary story Thoricus was a place where a mortal called Cephalus

was taken up to the gods and that the "hollow pear tree" may mark the spot where Persephone was abducted by Hades and taken down to the underworld (i.e., they are references to places where the gods took some mortal being away).

57. Demeter was a goddess protecting crops. She was worshipped in various manifestations (Black Demeter, Green Demeter, Yellow Demeter—symbolizing the different stages of the crop cycle—black earth, the first appearance of a young crop, and harvest time).

58. Zeus is traditionally a god associated with the sky and heaven, but some Greek cities worshipped Zeus as a god of earth or of under the earth.

59. Some lines have been apparently been lost from this speech.

60. Ismene's objections to Antigone's desire to visit Oedipus' resting place are that it opposes Oedipus' express wishes (and is therefore not lawful) and that no one knows where the burial site is.

61. Jebb questions whether in this exchange (up to the arrival of Theseus) there might be some confusion in the way speeches have traditionally been assigned, since Antigone's sudden and urgent concern about where she is to go now does not seem to fit her obviously strong preoccupation with visiting her father's burial place as soon as possible. The speeches given to Antigone here seem much more appropriate coming from Ismene, who is clearly wondering about where she is to find a home now that Oedipus is dead. I have made no changes to the traditional arrangement, but I find Jebb's observations quite attractive (and I would probably try them out if I were mounting a production of the play).

62. Since with the death of Oedipus in Athens, the gods have seen to it that he gets what he most desires and that the Athenians obtain a guarantee of political security, there is no reason to feel sad. To do so would be to go against what the gods have established (and thus invite their angry punishment).

63. The "god there" is (one assumes) the divine spirit who took Oedipus away. Horkos (meaning Oath) is a god who serves Zeus by witnessing oaths and punishing perjury. I have added a line in English to clarify his function.

Oedipus at Colonus

Oedipus at Colonus

Oedipus at Colonus

www.ingramcontent.com/pod-product-compliance
Lightning Source LLC
Chambersburg PA
CBHW060924040426
42445CB00011B/786
9781940997896